A

RIVER

IN

DARKNESS

A

RIVER

IN

DARKNESS

One Man's Escape
from North Korea

Masaji Ishikawa

*Translated by Risa Kobayashi
and Martin Brown*

amazoncrossing

Previously published as 北朝鮮大脱出 地獄からの生還 by 新潮社 in Japan in 2000. Translated from Japanese by Risa Kobayashi and Martin Brown. First published in English by AmazonCrossing in 2017.

Published by AmazonCrossing, Seattle

www.apub.com

Amazon, the Amazon logo, and AmazonCrossing are trademarks of Amazon.com, Inc., or its affiliates.

ISBN-13:9781503936904 (Hardcover)
ISBN-10:1503936902 (Hardcover)
ISBN-13: 9781542047197 (Paperback)
ISBN-10: 1542047196 (Paperback)

Cover design by Rachel Adam Rogers

Printed in the United States of America
First edition

A

RIVER

IN

DARKNESS

ABOUT THE AUTHOR

Masaji Ishikawa was born in 1947. His father was a Korean national residing in Japan. His mother was Japanese. In 1960, when he was thirteen years old, his family moved to the "promised land" of North Korea. In 1996, he made a desperate bid to escape from that hell on earth.

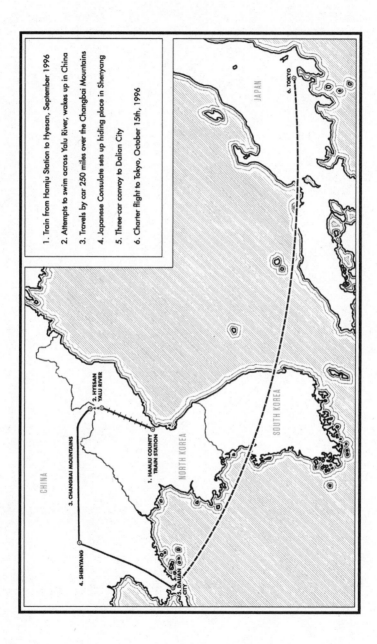

1. Train from Hamju Station to Hyesan, September 1996

2. Attempts to swim across Yalu River, wakes up in China

3. Travels by car 250 miles over the Changbai Mountains

4. Japanese Consulate sets up hiding place in Shenyang

5. Three-car convoy to Dalian City

6. Charter flight to Tokyo, October 15th, 1996

CHINA

3. CHANGBAI MOUNTAINS

4. SHENYANG

2. HYESAN
YALU RIVER

1. HAMJU COUNTY
TRAIN STATION

5. DALIAN
CITY

NORTH KOREA

SOUTH KOREA

JAPAN

6. TOKYO

PROLOGUE

What do I remember of that night? The night I escaped from North Korea? There are so many things that I *don't* remember, that I've put out of my mind forever . . . But I'll tell you what I do recall.

It's drizzling. But soon the drizzle turns to torrential rain. Sheets of rain so heavy, I'm soaked to the skin. I collapse under the shelter of a bush, utterly incapable of measuring the passage of time. I am weary to the core.

My legs have sunk into the mud, but somehow I crawl out from under the bush. Between the branches, I can see the Yalu River in front of me. But it's changed—now totally unrecognizable. This morning, kids were wading in what was little more than a stream. But the cascading downpour has turned it into an impassable torrent.

Across the river, about thirty yards away, I can make out China, shrouded in mist. Thirty yards—the distance between life and death. I shiver. I know that countless North Koreans have stood here before me, gazing across at China under the cover of darkness, memories of the people they've just left behind swirling through their minds. Those people, like the ones I've left, were starving. What else could they do? I stare into the torrent and wonder how many of them succeeded.

Then again, what difference does it make? If I remain in North Korea, I'll die of starvation. It's as simple as that. At least this way there's a chance—a chance I'll make it, that I will be able to rescue my family or at least help them somehow. My children have always been my reason for living. I'm no use to them if I'm dead. But I still can't believe what I'm about to do. How many days have passed since my decision to escape across the border and return to the country of my birth? I think it through.

Four days . . . It seems like a lifetime. Four days ago, I left my house. I looked into my wife's face, my children's faces, for what I knew could be the last time. I couldn't let myself indulge in that kind of thinking, though. If I was going to have any chance of helping them, I had to leave while I still had the strength to escape. Or die trying.

And what have I eaten since? A few husks of sweet corn, kernels not included. An odd apple core. Some scraps I've scrounged from others' trash.

I look for the guards I know are lurking every fifty yards or so on the riverbank. I'm prepared to die of utter exhaustion or to drown in my attempt to cross the river. But I won't allow the guards to catch me. Anything but that. I plunge into the river.

The last words I spoke to my family still ring in my ears. *If I succeed in escaping, somehow or other, no matter what it takes, I'll get you there too.*

CHAPTER 1

You don't choose to be born. You just are. And your birth is your destiny, some say. I say the hell with that. And I should know. I was born not just once but five times. And five times I learned the same lesson. Sometimes in life, you have to grab your so-called destiny by the throat and wring its neck.

My Japanese name is Masaji Ishikawa, and my Korean name is Do Chan-sun. I was born (for the first time) in the neighborhood of Mizonokuchi in the city of Kawasaki, just south of Tokyo. It was my misfortune to be born between two worlds—to a Korean father and a Japanese mother. Mizonokuchi is an area of gently sloping hills that now grows crowded on the weekends with visitors from Tokyo and Yokohama seeking an escape from the city and some fresh air. But sixty years ago, when I was a child, it consisted of little more than a few farms, with irrigation canals that led from the Tama River running between them.

Back then, the irrigation canals were used not just for farming but also for household tasks like laundry and washing dishes. As a boy, I spent long summer days playing in the canals. I'd lie in a big washtub and float on the water all afternoon, basking in the sunshine and watching the clouds cross the sky. To my child's eye, the slow movement of those drifting clouds made the sky look like a vast expanse of sea. I wondered what would happen if I let my body drift with the clouds.

Could I cross the sea and reach a country I'd never known? Never even heard of? I thought of endless opportunities in my future. I wanted to help poor people—families like mine—become richer so that they could have the means to enjoy their lives. And I wanted the world to be peaceful. I dreamed one day that I would be the prime minister of Japan. How little I knew!

I used to climb a nearby hill and catch beetles in the early-morning dew. At festival time, I'd follow the portable shrine and the dance with the lion's mask. All my memories are sweet. My family was poor, but my childhood days in Mizonokuchi were the happiest of my life. Even now, when I think about my hometown, I can't stop the tears from welling up. I would give anything to go back to that happy time, to feel so innocent and full of hope once more.

On the outskirts of Mizonokuchi there used to be a village, home to two hundred or so Koreans. I found out later that most of them had been more or less dragged over from Korea—to work in the nearby munitions factory. My father, Do Sam-dal, was one of them. Born on a farm in the village of Bongchon-ri in what is now South Korea, he was commandeered—effectively kidnapped—at the age of fourteen and brought to Mizonokuchi.

But I didn't even know I had a father until I started elementary school. I have no earlier memories of him whatsoever. In fact, I first became conscious of my father's existence when my mother took me to a strange place, which I later discovered was a prison, to visit a man I didn't recognize. That's the day my mother told me who my father was. Eventually the man I'd seen through the window in the visitors' room showed up at our house. He was notorious in the area for being a rough fellow, and our relatives shunned him.

He was hardly ever at home, but whenever he *was* there, he spent the better part of his time slugging back strong-smelling liquor. He could polish off a couple liters of sake in short order. What was worse, drunk or not, he'd hit my mother whenever he was at home. My sisters were so frightened, they used to cower in the corner. I tried to stop him by clinging to his leg, but he always kicked me away. My mother tried not to cry out, so she bore the pain with clenched teeth. I felt helpless and scared for her but could do nothing. As time went on, I just did my best to stay out of his way—which wasn't hard since he never paid much attention to me. But it crossed my mind more than once that I'd come after him when I grew up.

My mother's name was Miyoko Ishikawa. She was born in 1925. Her parents ran a shop on the corner of the ancient shopping street, where they sold chickens. My grandmother, Hatsu, ran the shop, and her work was difficult and dirty. The chicken meat wasn't neatly cut up and packaged as it is today—nothing like that. Cages were strewn higgledy-piggledy in front of the shop, and when a customer appeared, my grandmother would remove a squawking chicken from its cage and slaughter it on the spot.

My grandmother suffered from asthma, so she often had coughing fits. Whenever she spotted me coming home from school or from playing somewhere, she'd arch her back and say, "Mabo, can you rub my back?" So I'd stroke and massage her small back for a few minutes. During those times together, she always said to me, "You're a kind boy. You mustn't be like your father. I just can't understand why your mother made the mistake of marrying him."

I could see why she used the word "mistake." The Ishikawa family was respected and went back a long way in the area. There were many branches of the Ishikawa family in Mizonokuchi. They and the rest of the local people formed a close-knit community. My grandfather, Shoukichi, died before I was born, but I was always told he was a good and gentle man who looked after his family and others in his community. He sent my mother to a girls' high school and encouraged her to learn how to sew. Though the family couldn't be called wealthy, he did his best to provide his children with an education of sorts.

My mother was a woman of strong character. She had an oval face that was beautiful in its way. My father, on the other hand, had sharp, razorlike eyes, a well-built body, and muscular shoulders. I don't know what my mother saw in him—perhaps she was attracted to his confidence and survival instincts. I do know that the local community was stunned when they started living together. Behind their backs, people called them "Beauty and the Beast" and wondered why she'd married such a terrible man.

My grandmother once said to me, "Koreans are barbarians." I loved her, but I resented her remark. Though I felt Japanese—and felt it with complete conviction—I was half-Korean, as she knew perfectly well. My mother's elder brothers, Shiro and Tatsukichi, occasionally made similar remarks. They'd been conscripted to serve in the Japanese army in Manchuria and always described Koreans as poor and unkempt, like a bunch of gorillas. They never had the guts to say anything like that in front of my father, of course. But when my father wasn't around, Shiro would often say, "Miyoko had better divorce him as soon as possible. Koreans are just rotten to the core." Though I always felt a twinge of discomfort when he said such things, I couldn't help but agree with them. I had a strong sense of revulsion toward my father, who certainly lived up to the barbaric reputation of Koreans whenever he beat my mother. Given that we watched him torment her day after day—and that he frightened me and my sisters to death in the process—it was hardly surprising that I, like my grandmother, grew to dislike Koreans.

My father used to strut about the neighborhood with twenty or thirty Korean followers in tow. He was one of the top dogs in the Korean community, and he enjoyed picking a fight with any Japanese who got on his nerves. He didn't care who it was. Special policeman? Sure. Military policeman? Bring it on. Koreans could depend on him for protection, but he scared the daylights out of Japanese people.

My father always insisted on doing things his own way. After the end of the Second World War, he opened a black-market street-side stall with several of his cronies. They sold canned food produced in the munitions factory where my father used to work, and sugar, flour, ship's biscuits, clothes, and other items procured illegally from American GIs. One day my dad and his buddies got into a huge brawl with American soldiers over the merchandise he was selling. He was notorious for a reason.

Not that my father had many options. The Japanese defeat in World War II left 2.4 million Koreans stranded in Japan. They belonged to neither the winning nor the losing side, and they had no place to go. Once freed, they were simply thrown onto the streets. Desperate and impoverished, with no way to make a living, they attacked the trucks containing food intended for members of the imperial Japanese armed forces and sold the booty on the black market. Even those who'd never been violent before had little choice but to turn into outlaws.

In a strange sort of way, all this illegality actually set these people free. During the war, they had only two grim choices: they could either become soldiers in their enemy's army or slave away as civilian war workers. The soldiers would be sent to the front to be used as human shields against the shells. The laborers would be worked to the bone— and sometimes death—in coal mines or munitions factories. The life of an outlaw was a kind of liberation.

At some point, my father joined what was then known as the General Association of Koreans in Japan, later to be known as the League of Korean Residents in Japan. This community for Koreans in Japan supported the principle of friendship between Japanese and Korean people and strove to help Koreans live a stable and regular life in Japan. But it wasn't as simple as it sounded. Ever since before the Second World War, many Koreans with "permanent resident" status in Japan had respected the Communist Party. Communist policies were anti-imperialist, and the party campaigned for the rights of Korean permanent residents. After the war, not long after the Association was formed, a famous Communist by the name of Kim Chon-hae was released from prison, along with several other Communist Party members. These individuals had remained defiant in prison and had refused to change their thinking. After their release, they had a powerful influence on the Association, which naturally became more left-wing as a result. But the fundamental principle governing my father's behavior at the time had nothing to do with socialism. The important thing for him was nationalism.

From my perspective, there wasn't much difference between a socialist movement, a nationalist movement, and a brutal brawl in the black market. All of these people had a couple of things in common. They all had their own personal histories in Japan—and they were all poor. They just wanted to assert their own existence. And that meant fighting however they could to gain some kind of power.

Within the Association, my father became known as "Tiger." No surprise there. He had his "action force" of loyal street fighters, in reality a group of guys who'd get together in front of the old shop, make a fire in an iron basket, and slug back liquor all day. I don't know if they were discussing troubles in the black market or just waiting for their "action force" to be needed, but whenever something happened and their presence was called for, they'd spring into action and rush to the scene.

In the end, everything fell apart for my father. The General Association of Korean Residents was deemed a terrorist group and ordered to disband in 1949. The League of Koreans in Japan served as a replacement for many, but times had changed. By then, public order had been restored, and someone like my father, an impulsive and poorly educated street fighter, simply wasn't needed anymore. What the newly launched League really needed at that time were skilled administrators—there was no place for my father, who couldn't even read, in the new order. I can't help but wonder now whether his rejection from that group ultimately made him more vulnerable to the promises he started hearing about a great life to be had in North Korea . . .

These days I find more and more memories coming back to me. Sometimes, I wish they wouldn't.

I had three younger sisters—Eiko, Hifumi, and Masako—but we hardly ever lived together in Japan. Because our family was so poor, we were split up and sent to our relatives' houses so they could share the task of taking care of us, thereby lightening the burden. That changed in my final year of elementary school when we all moved to Nakano in Tokyo. My father had decided to get a job in the construction industry. Or so he said. I do know that we had to move in a great rush. We didn't even have time to say goodbye to our neighbors, and we had to leave our beloved grandmother behind.

Although I was initially worried about leaving everything I knew and moving to a place that I'd never seen, I was happy with our new life at first. We started living like a real family. We got up together in the morning and went to bed together at night. We ate dinner together, and we had family routines. Those little things meant so much to me. After all, the little things usually tie families together with the bonds of familial love. But that happy time was destroyed almost before it started. It wasn't long before my father's violence returned—worse than ever.

Within weeks of our arrival, my father started drinking again, as soon as he returned home at the end of the day. And he went on drinking until his face settled into a dark scowl. When that happened, my mother would sequester my sisters and me in the adjoining room. We'd stand there helplessly and listen to the inevitable unraveling. The vicious sound of his voice as he ranted at our mother. The sound of his hitting her. The sound of his trying to stifle her tearful cries. The same thing happened night after night after night. I often couldn't understand what he was saying to her, but whatever it was, she never seemed to resist him. She just cried. Several times, I tried to burst into the room to stop my father. I even bit his leg once. But he just kicked me to the ground. My mother would lie over me, protecting me with her body. Finally, my father would get bored or so drunk, he'd stagger out of the house and disappear into the night. And my mother, my sisters, and I would sit on the floor, weeping silently, huddled together.

One night, one of the neighbors heard her screams and intervened. My father was caught off guard for a moment, but soon he seized the guy by the neck, forced him against the wall, and beat him senseless. No one ever came to our house after that.

It just got worse from there. When my father returned home late at night, he'd wake my mother up, just so that he could beat her yet again. And every night, I was terrified when I saw his maniacal face. It was like looking into the face of a demon. I couldn't get to sleep. I just kept seeing that face. And if I *did* fall asleep, I'd have nightmares about it.

Then came the worst night of all. It was autumn. I was twelve or thirteen. My father arrived home blind drunk, as usual. But this time, he didn't say anything. He went to the kitchen and returned with a kitchen knife. He pressed it to my mother's neck and forced her outside. I knew I had to follow them.

I hid behind a bush and watched as my father forced my mother up a steep hill pocked with craters. It had been quarried for earth and sand for use in the construction industry. I followed them in the darkness as my father forced my mother to the edge of a steep drop. I trembled with fear at the sight of the knife glinting in the dark night. He uttered a loud yell and then gave her a hard push. She howled as she stumbled backward, then toppled over the edge. My father just stood there for a moment, the knife still gleaming in his hand as he looked down from the top. Then he stomped off in the direction of our house.

I raced to the hill, to the edge where I had seen my mother tumble. I couldn't make out how high it was, but I jumped over the edge anyway. Luckily, the soil was soft, and I wasn't hurt. My mother lay there like a broken doll, her blouse soaked in blood. I hauled her up and held her, screaming, "You mustn't die! Don't die on me! You can't go and die on me now!" Finally she regained consciousness. As I hugged her, she said, "Masabo, I have to leave. He'll kill me if I don't. You have to be strong." I felt helpless and bereft as I clung to her. She was everything to me—the only kind person in my life—but I knew she had no choice.

I helped her limp along through the darkness. I burst through the door at the hospital near the railway station and woke up the doctor. He was a kind man who treated her injuries without hesitation. Miraculously, she didn't need a single stitch.

Later we sat on a bench near the station together in silence, waiting for the first train of the day. Suddenly my mother spoke.

"Don't worry," she said. "I'll work hard and save some money. And then I'll come back for you and your sisters, so wait for me till then."

And then she just wept, very quietly. Her face was thinner and paler than I'd ever seen it. She looked empty. I wanted to be strong. But there she was, covered in cuts and bruises, and there was nothing I could do about it. So I too began to cry, from sheer frustration and despair. Why did she have to go through such a terrible ordeal? Why did my father hate her so? She was so gentle and kind. It made no sense to me.

When the train pulled into the station, my mother stood up, gave me a quick hug, and walked away. She turned and waved to me from the ticket barrier. Then I plodded back to our house. I felt numb, bewildered, and utterly alone.

My father acted as if nothing had happened. To make matters worse, his mistress moved into the house shortly after my mother left. Her name was Kanehara, and she was Korean, like my father. She was wicked and cruel, especially toward my younger sisters, but my father never struck Kanehara. Not once. In fact, to my surprise, they seemed quite besotted with each other. They were constantly laughing and smiling at each other. Their behavior made me sick. I tried to be strong, but my sisters missed my mother desperately and cried every night. When they cried, Kanehara would slap them and berate them, which only made them miss my mother even more.

I gave up going to school and instead scoured Tokyo every day, looking for my mother. Every morning, I boarded the train and walked the streets for hours on end. This went on for half a year at least. I painstakingly searched every restaurant in the area, determined not to give up, and my efforts finally paid off. One afternoon, I spotted her through a restaurant window. Unable to move, I watched her as she scrubbed a table. Then I started to cry. I must have looked pretty suspicious to the restaurant owner, but he beckoned me in. I ran straight to my mother and hugged her.

The restaurant owner kindly gave me something to eat. And suddenly, the words came gushing out. I couldn't stop talking. I told my mother all about Kanehara—how she was living with us, and how she was treating my sisters, and how they missed her, and on and on. She smiled gently. "Be patient for a little while longer," she said. Then she gave me her necklace and gold ring. "If you have any trouble," she said, "take these to a pawnbroker. But don't talk to your father about me, okay? Don't tell him you've seen me. Don't tell him where I am."

Now that I had found my mother, I started going to school again and went to see her almost every afternoon as soon as classes finished. Sometimes, on the weekend or on public holidays, I took my younger sisters with me. The restaurant owner was very kind to us. I guess he knew our story. As for Kanehara, she could hit me all she liked because I truly believed that, one day soon, my mother would come back and rescue us.

Looking back on it all, I think I can make sense of my father's frame of mind at the time. But I can't forgive him for what he did.

In his heyday, he had twenty or thirty followers. And he was the boss. The main man. The godfather. In the black market, your birth and background meant nothing. You could be an ex-military man. You could be nobility. Japanese . . . Korean . . . It didn't matter. Your birth or background meant nothing. All that mattered was your physical strength, and my father knew how to live by violence. But later on, when the war ended and everything returned to normal, his physical strength no longer had any value. Suddenly, nationality and background meant everything. And in this new hierarchy, my father was nothing. He had no family connections by birth. Worse, he was Korean. That made it tough to get a job. When the General Association of Korean Residents was outlawed, his leadership role in his "action force" vanished. As his ex-comrades rose to lofty heights in the League of Koreans in Japan, he remained scrabbling about in the dirt with no prospects. So he took it out on my mother. Her family owned property of a kind, and she herself had a reasonable education—things he was hungry for but could never obtain himself. So she bore the brunt of all his anger toward the world. At first, I wondered why he never hit Kanehara. My guess is that it was because she was Korean and didn't serve as a constant reminder of all that he couldn't have.

One thing I learned around this time was that while some people— people like my father—just like to show off their physical strength, others have a particular reason for being violent.

In my final year of elementary school, my father decided that I should go to a Korean junior high school, even though I didn't speak Korean. I didn't want to go, but I was too scared to oppose his wishes, so off I went.

Most of us at school came from poor families. Our poverty stemmed from racial discrimination, pure and simple. Most students never actively vented their frustration about this—they were just too busy trying to get by—but that didn't mean they took everything lying down. My schoolmates often had run-ins with Japanese people when they were playing outside or on their way home from school. Over time, they all came to associate racial discrimination with violence. And the logic was straightforward. If someone hit you, you didn't turn the other cheek. You hit them back. Twice as hard.

I felt torn as I watched my classmates. Now that I'd shared a classroom with them for a while, I felt a growing kinship with them. I'd come to realize that my grandparents and other relatives were wrong. Koreans were nothing like the monsters they'd described. Oh sure, they were rough—how could they *not* be—but they were also warm and kind. Although I still kept my distance from most of them, I started talking to a boy named Kan Te-son, who sat next to me in class. The rest of us had closely cropped hair, but Son's hair was kind of unkempt, despite school rules. His hair resembled a mane that had earned him the nickname "Lion."

After Lion learned about my family situation, he invited me to come home with him one day. We walked through the maze of a Korean neighborhood near a confectionary factory, and the sweet smell of candy permeated the air. When we arrived at his house, his mother immediately asked me if I was hungry. A moment later, she rushed into the kitchen and reemerged with rice, Korean pickles, and several other dishes. The table was soon filled with food.

She kept saying, "Eat more!" even though my mouth was full and I was practically choking on the rice I was wolfing down. Lion and his mother watched me, and I couldn't help noticing their smiles. I'd experienced maternal love, and of course I loved my sisters dearly, but this was the first time I'd felt real affection from people not related to me. Their warmth and empathy were palpable. To tell you the truth, I was so stunned, I could barely swallow. From then on, Lion's house was the only place I could ever relax. Even as my life took its twists and turns, I never forgot his family's kindness.

Once Lion and I had become friends, I felt more capable of talking to my classmates. But most of my classes were still totally incomprehensible to me since they were taught in Korean. Math made sense, as did science up to a point. But the rest was just gibberish. There were others like me who couldn't speak Korean at all. And you know what? Some teachers *bent the rules* and explained things to us in Japanese. Dissidents!

We were taught that Kim Il-sung was "the king who liberated Korea from colonialism." He'd waged a war against US imperialists and their South Korean lackeys—and had won. It was thoroughly drummed into us that Kim Il-sung was an invincible general made of steel. I could tell the teachers were proud of his role as the Great Leader of an emerging nation.

Around this period, Japan was hit by recession. Many companies went bankrupt, and unemployment rose sharply. Korean people were at the bottom of the pile, and circumstances that had merely been difficult before soon became dire for many families. Meanwhile, in North Korea, Kim Il-sung proclaimed he was building a socialist utopia. It was called the Chollima Movement. Like the rest of us, our teachers were living in poverty. So they grasped at straws. There was this land, this "promised land," a "paradise on earth," a "land of milk and honey." In their desperation, they fell for these claims—and passed these lies on to us. I listened to what they said with half an ear at best. Oh sure, there was this "paradise on earth" across the sea, but the here and now was all that mattered to me. How could I improve my life right now? Demonstrations were erupting in the streets, my family was barely scraping by, and we were constantly on edge. Added to that, Kanehara was still living with us, and my sisters and I were still sneaking off to see my mother every weekend. Given everything that was going on all around me daily, it was hard to care much about the "paradise" of North Korea.

One day, about a year after my mother ran away, I came home to find a row of shoes lined up just inside the front door. I was stunned by what I found inside: some guys were berating my father and—most important—they were not being beaten to death. There was only one answer: they had to be bigwigs in the League. I entered the room unobtrusively and listened to their conversation. One of them said, "Look. If you can't clean up your act with regard to your wife, we'll break off our friendship with you." Another said, "We'll take things up with the League. Then you'll be screwed." One by one, they all laid into him. They thumped the tatami mats and raised their voices as they asked him to reflect on what he'd done and set out all the sordid details of his life. After an hour or so, satisfied that they had made their point, they all got up and left. My father and Kanehara also left, but I had no idea where they slunk off to. My father returned later that night alone. I do not know where Kanehara went. I never saw her again.

A few days later, some guys affiliated with the League showed up at our door with my mother. I was so stunned by this turn of events, I could only look on in amazement. One of the fellows from the League prostrated himself in front of my mother. "Your husband has promised he'll mend his ways. Are you willing to start over with him? This isn't only about you. Think of the children," he said. My mother was dazed and speechless, but in the end, she agreed to return. Although my sisters shrieked with delight and excitement, I was worried sick. All I could think about was that my father would start beating her again—it was just a question of when. But a day went by. Nothing. A week, then a month. Nothing. He never hit her again. Men from the League kept stopping by our house to make sure.

It didn't end there. They also took my father to task about his lack of work. They'd come in and scold him relentlessly about it. "Look! You don't have a job. And what do you do? You get drunk all the time and make your wife's life a misery. But if you went *there* . . . there are jobs galore! Think of it! You'll get to send your kids to university." I didn't know where "there" was, but they repeatedly urged him to go "back" there. They talked and talked, sometimes till midnight and beyond. I could hear every word they said through the thin sliding door that separated my room from theirs. They were clearly discussing something that would change my life completely. Irrevocably. I was scared out of my wits at the thought of what it might be. Then, lo and behold, the same thing came up at school. "North Korea is your country. It's a paradise on earth. This is your chance. Go home!" But North Korea wasn't my country. It had nothing to do with me. Why was my father being urged to "return" there?

Kim Il-sung barked on about it in a speech we listened to at school on September 8, 1958, if my memory serves me correctly. Something along the lines of "Our fellow countrymen living in Japan have no rights and are discriminated against. Because of that, they are suffering from the hardships of poverty, and they want to return to their mother country. We would like to welcome them back. The government of the People's Republic will ensure that they can start a new life when they come home. We will guarantee their living conditions." The expression "return to North Korea" still didn't make sense to me. My father was from the southern part of Korea, not from North Korea. North Korea didn't exist when my father was born. Why would he "return" to a place he'd never known?

After Kim Il-sung's statement, the General Association of Korean Residents started a mass repatriation campaign in the guise of humanitarianism. The following year, 1959, the Japanese Red Cross Society and the Korean Red Cross Society secretly negotiated a "Return Agreement" in Calcutta. Four months later, the first shipload of returnees left the Japanese port of Niigata. Shortly after that, people affiliated with the League of Koreans in Japan started showing up on our doorstep, eager to persuade us to make the journey. They were all in favor of the mass repatriation.

Did the International Committee of the Red Cross know anything about this? Did the United States? The UN? Yes, yes, and yes. And what did they do about it? Nothing.

In the early days of the so-called repatriation, some seventy thousand people left Japan and crossed the sea to North Korea. With the exception of a brief three-and-a-half-year hiatus, the process continued until 1984. During this period, some one hundred thousand Koreans and two thousand Japanese wives crossed over to North Korea. That's one hell of a mass migration. In fact, it was the first (and only) time in history that so many people from a capitalist country had moved to a socialist country.

The Japanese government actively promoted the repatriation, supposedly on humanitarian grounds. But in my opinion, what they were actually pursuing was opportunism of the most vile and cynical kind. Look at the facts. During the period of the Japanese Empire, thousands upon thousands of Koreans had been brought to Japan against their will to serve as slave laborers and, later, cannon fodder. Now, the government was afraid that these Koreans and their families, discriminated against and poverty-stricken in the postwar years, might become a source of social unrest. Sending them back to Korea was a solution to a problem. Nothing more.

From the North Korean government's point of view, their country desperately needed rebuilding after the Korean War. What could be more convenient than an influx of workers? Kim Il-sung was desperate to prove to the world that the Democratic Republic was superior to South Korea. The prospect of thousands of Koreans returning home to serve as foot soldiers in the Great March Forward (as I call it) fueled his maniacal dreams.

So yes, the mass repatriation was great news for both governments—the perfect win-win situation for everyone except the real human beings involved.

We were bombarded with a constant stream of infantile, almost hysterical pronouncements. "Enjoy working and studying in North Korea!" and "North Korea is a paradise on earth!" The League and the mass media were equally to blame. The bigwigs in the League were simply delusional, the journalists spectacularly naive. Oh sure, they felt guilty about Japan's colonial past, but this guilt, far from sharpening their judgment, clouded their thinking and befuddled their critical faculties. I mean, this was the second half of the twentieth century, for pity's sake, and they still saw communism as the road to utopia. I wonder if any of the people spouting these messages ever really grasped, in later years, the depths of misery for which they were responsible.

Having said that, I'm not convinced that naive utopianism was the actual driving force behind people's decision to migrate. For most displaced Koreans living in Japan at the time, the key point was a much simpler promise: "If you come back to your homeland, the government will guarantee you a stable life and a first-class education for your children." For the countless Koreans who were unemployed, underpaid, and laboring away at whatever odd jobs they could get, the abstract promises of socialism held far less sway than the hope for a stable life and a bright future for their children.

Early one evening in 1959, when I walked in the door from school, my father announced, "We're going back to my country." I shook with anger and shock. "No way!" I said. "I don't want to go!" My heart was racing, and I turned to my sisters and my mother for help. My sisters weren't old enough to grasp what the conversation was about, so they just listened to us timidly as my father went on. "What do we have here to eat? Practically nothing. But if we go *there*, we'll have a steady life—something we've never had here!" My mother broke in, her voice trembling. "But I can't speak Korean. How on earth am I going to live?" She sounded terrified, and I held out some hope that she'd stand up to him. But I also noticed she didn't say outright that she wouldn't go.

My grandmother was furious when my mother and I went to tell her what my father had proposed. Apoplectic. "That's a terrible idea! You can't possibly be serious. All Koreans are barbarians, just like your husband. Besides, you and your children are Japanese. The North Koreans will hate you and abuse you. I just know this will end badly." I'd never seen her as angry as she was that day.

When we got home, some creeps from the League were hovering about.

They came to see my mother every day and gradually wore her down with their promises. They said things like, "If you go there, you'll never have another quarrel. Your children will be able to go to school for free. And after three years, you'll be able to come back to Japan for a visit." Wheedling creeps. I hated them.

And in the end, they won. The bastards won. My mother agreed to go to North Korea with my father. I was astounded. And distraught. What was my mother thinking? Why on earth did she decide to go with him? Was it love? After all he'd put her through? Or had she agreed out of some strange sense of duty? Did she actually buy the promises of a better life? I'll never know.

Our departure was scheduled for January 1960. When the day finally came, my father, my mother, my sisters, and I left our home for the last time and made our way to Shinagawa Station, where a large crowd had gathered. Though I knew better than to expect them, I scanned the crowd for a glimpse of my grandmother and my uncles and cousins, but they were nowhere to be seen. My grandmother had announced that she was done with my mother and would never speak to her again. I had nonetheless hoped that one of them—any of them—would come to say goodbye. A brass band played and marched in stiff, heroic formation as an earsplitting din blasted out of a speaker above the crowd. Everywhere people shouted, "Hooray!"

My friend Lion pushed his way through the crowd. He grabbed me by the shoulders and shook me, his face streaming with tears.

"Are you really going?"

"I'll write to you. And I promise to come back someday."

That was all I could manage to say. My stomach was twisted in knots. So many emotions were churning inside me as we boarded the train. When I looked back at him from my seat, his face was pale. I suddenly knew I'd never see him again.

When the train started moving, a great cacophony of cheering and screaming seemed to come from everywhere. All at once the adults on the train started crying. I wondered why. After all, they were going back to their homeland, so why were they sad? It seemed to portend bad things to come.

CHAPTER 2

We shuffled off the train and were ushered into the chaotic and crowded Japanese Red Cross headquarters, where we spent the next three nights. We were then shunted and rubber-stamped through the official process of "repatriation" to a country that none of us had ever lived in. Some Japanese wives discarded their Japanese passports when presented with Korean papers, but my mother kept hers. There was a sentence, buried somewhere in the paperwork, that stated, "Once you have settled in North Korea, you will not be allowed to return to Japan without official Japanese authorization." I tried to convince myself that since I was Japanese by birth, it wouldn't be a problem for me to come back someday. But as we went through the various bureaucratic steps, I couldn't help but feel an overwhelming sense of dread.

Finally we were bused to the port, and we clambered aboard an ancient-looking Soviet passenger ship, the *Kuririon*. The Red Cross staff struggled with the staggering amount of paperwork and simply let people traipse on board. The ship set off shortly after we embarked. There was no returning. I stared forlornly back at Japan as we left the port of Niigata, then watched the dull, leaden waves crashing against the ship's bow. The spray spewed and foamed and soaked the Soviet seamen working on deck, who wore only T-shirts despite the cold wind that lashed the Sea of Japan.

I looked around. Incredibly, some of my fellow passengers had boarded the ship without any luggage at all. What on earth were they thinking? I remembered the ridiculous public notice issued by the League of Koreans in Japan: "If you go to North Korea, you will be able to obtain everything you need." That was blind faith for you.

After two long days at sea, I was in my bunk when someone called out that we were approaching the North Korean port of Chongjin. We all rushed up on deck. I spotted a mountain off in the distance. It looked miserable and bare. There was hardly a tree to be seen. Someone cried, "Hooray to Grand Marshal Kim Il-sung!" Some of the other passengers got caught up in the mood and joined in with more cheering. But another sound welled up from others, a sort of combined groan and scream that quickly grew louder and more terrifying. An elderly man standing next to me clutched the ship's rail. "This is . . ." His words trailed off. "This isn't what I expected," he gasped. His body grew rigid, and his knuckles turned as white as his ashen face. His ghostlike appearance made me shudder. I huddled close to my sister Eiko, for warmth, but also for some measure of comfort. As I stared out at that barren mountain, I couldn't help but wonder what would become of us.

As we approached the port, I noticed several rusty ships anchored nearby. They looked completely abandoned. No cargo was waiting to be unloaded. No longshoremen were on the quay. A ghost port. The bald hills in the background made everything look even more desolate and bleak.

An orchestra was playing on the dock, its music thin and haunting. Welcome to North Korea! I remembered the ghastly brass band back in Niigata—its jaunty, preposterous, inane pomposity. And now here was this sad orchestra, scraping away in the icy wind. As the ship edged closer to the quay, I saw that the players were all schoolgirls. Although it was midwinter, they wore little more than the thin jacket of the Korean national costume. The sharp wind blew in my eyes. Then I took a second look. Their faces. Their phony smiles. You must have seen them on TV. Those grotesque displays of schoolgirls—automata wheeled out in Pyongyang to celebrate the birthday of the Dear Leader or some other such dismal anniversary. And there they were, in prototype. The rictus grins of the brainwashed. Of course, I didn't fully understand what I was seeing at the time, but even then, I knew it was nonsense.

When we pulled up to the quay, several North Koreans came on board to help with our disembarkation. Their clothes, their shoes, everything about them, made it clear at once that these denizens of paradise were infinitely poorer than we'd ever been during our tough life in Japan. As we trudged down the gangway, I kept thinking about one of the documents we'd received. It referred to some kind of "application for return" and said something to the effect of, "If you wish to return to Japan at any stage, even if you are on the verge of entering North Korea, inform any member of the Red Cross staff around you immediately." I looked around frantically for a Red Cross employee, but my father placed his palm against my shoulder blades and pushed me forward. I had no choice but to keep walking down that gangway.

Born again.

We were shepherded onto buses and taken to reception centers in the city. I stared out the window, feeling desolate as I looked for anything that might give me hope. I saw only a few houses on the way into town. The landscape was dreary, still scarred by bomb craters left over from the Korean War. Once we arrived, we were interviewed by officials who decided each person's future occupation and accommodation. Just like that. I couldn't believe how casual my father was. When he was asked where he wanted to go, he simply said, "Anywhere is okay. I don't know the names of any places in North Korea. I'm happy to go wherever." He was so confident and optimistic, but I couldn't believe he had just placed us at the mercy of the officials.

My mother, however, was racked with anxiety. I'll never forget the look of sheer panic and terror on her face. "What's going to happen to us?" she asked, her voice shaking. "Never mind. It'll be okay," my father kept saying. I kept silent. How could he be so confident that everything would be fine? Looking back at that day, I think language played a role. At last, he could speak his native Korean again. At last he belonged. This sense of relief seemed to seep into the rest of his thinking. I could see him relaxing into his mother tongue, and this gave him confidence about everything else.

Of course, like my mother, I was anxious about the future, but for me—a fast-growing thirteen-year-old—the most alarming thing was when we sat down to our first meal. I couldn't believe the dish that appeared in front of me. They served us dog meat. Yes, dog meat. The stench was overpowering. We were ravenous, so we held our noses, but even then we gagged. I really tried to overcome my nausea, but none of us could get so much as a bite down. Except my father.

It was strictly forbidden for us to leave the reception center. So there we were—the beneficiaries of smug humanitarianism—prisoners in paradise on earth. Each family was given one room about six tatami mats wide. Icy gusts of wind blew into the room through the flimsy walls, and gravel pelted our cheeks. That first night, as we all lay side by side, shivering on the freezing-cold floor, I wondered what was going to become of us. My sisters just kept calling out to me softly, plaintively, "Brother! Brother!" They were exhausted, trembling with cold, and scared. I wanted to comfort them but couldn't think of much to say.

We spent several weeks in this state of limbo, sitting in the cold day after day and shivering on the floor night after night, fearful of the future and uncertain what awaited us. I tried not to think about anything—to ignore my memories of the life I'd left behind and not imagine what our life here would look like.

A few weeks later, our destiny was determined. Our future home was to be in the village of Dong Chong-ri. I was nervous about this place I'd never heard of, but figured it had to be an improvement over the confines of the reception center. The journey took about twelve hours by steam train and another hour by oxcart. When we pulled slowly into the snowbound village, the oxcart came to a stop and we clambered down. My youngest sister, Masako, fell into the snow and began to cry. Soon she was wailing uncontrollably. She'd somehow withstood the horrors of our situation until that moment, but her tumble into the snow was the last straw. She'd just turned six, and her whole little life had been turned upside down in a few short weeks.

She kept wailing, "I want to go home!" as tears streamed down her cheeks. I was stunned when my father picked her up to soothe her. I'd never seen him show any fatherly affection before. He spoke to her softly and tried to calm her down as our guide led us down the road. I looked around at the ramshackle cottages with their thatched roofs sprinkled with snow. It sounds picturesque. But it wasn't. It was desolate.

The house that we were destined to call home was being used as a party office. It was the village's only building with a tiled roof. Our guide became excited, almost hysterical, as he pointed it out. Apparently, it was "a great honor to live in such a house." I looked at the thing in all its jerry-rigged glory, its walls riddled with cracks. I was puzzled. Did he *really* believe what he was saying? If so, I could almost have wept for him. Except that I was the one who had to live there.

A belligerent-looking woman was waiting for us by the door. She spoke to us in a hectoring, hysterical tone that was to become very familiar to me in the years to come. I later discovered that she was the chairperson of the local Democratic Women's Union. She'd dragged over some of our neighbors to welcome us. They were waiting inside. As soon as we crossed the threshold, she launched into a speech.

"These people were *bullied* in Japan, but thanks to the warmth and kindness of Grand Marshal Kim Il-sung, they could come back to their mother country!"

I couldn't help but notice that our future neighbors paid little attention to her words and were busy staring at us—ogling our watches and bicycles and the few other things we'd managed to bring with us. The lady turned to me. "I'll take you to school tomorrow, so be ready!" she said. And with that, she and the neighbors all left the house.

The lights appeared to be on, but the bulbs emitted only a thin and feeble glow. I didn't know about low voltage at the time. I looked around for gas points, but there weren't any. I couldn't even find a cold-water tap. I looked out the window. And there it was, about thirty yards away. A well.

My mother was distraught. Like me, she couldn't believe what she was seeing.

"How are we ever going to live here?"

The bleak walls echoed her words. I felt numb, overwhelmed, unable to think or feel anything. After the long journey, I lay down on a mat and tried to sleep. I tossed and turned and woke up exhausted and disoriented.

True to her word, the chairperson of the Democratic Women's Union came to collect me the following morning for my first day at school in North Korea. She turned up with her daughter, who proudly announced that she was the "scout leader." Although I couldn't speak much Korean at the time, I vaguely understood what she was talking about. I just said, "Good morning" and followed them. There were no first-day-of-school photographs for the family archive.

When I walked in, I saw about a hundred pupils and teachers gathered in a single room. I greeted them in my clumsy Korean.

"Thank you for welcoming me."

"Japanese bastard!" someone muttered.

And then everyone seemed to be whispering the words. "Japanese bastard!"

I was mortified. I felt the heat rising to my face. I wished I could disappear.

The pupils started pointing at my plastic shoes and other things they didn't approve of.

"Look at his bag!"

"He's wearing a watch!"

"Japanese bastard!"

I noticed that they didn't have bags themselves but simply wrapped their stuff in a cloth. I resolved to do the same from then on.

After this welcome, I watched as twenty pupils put on a play. It was a crude piece of propaganda that portrayed my life up to that point. According to the play, I'd led a hard life in Japan, but thanks to the kind efforts of the Workers' Party of Korea and the good old League of Koreans, I'd been able to "return" to my "mother country." When it was over, everyone clapped rapturously. I clapped too, just to be polite.

School was difficult, not because of my studies but because I could understand very little Korean. All I could do was vaguely deduce what people were saying from the context. I often got called "Japanese bastard" because I couldn't speak Korean. In hindsight, it was probably just as well that I couldn't answer back.

On my way home from school one day, I witnessed a fight among my schoolmates. I couldn't stand the sight of one guy getting beaten so badly, so I jumped on the bully. Although I was small, I was fearless and tough thanks to my father's genes and the tough Korean school I'd attended in Yokohama. To my surprise, I knocked him out. Then some man in uniform grabbed my collar. He came out with the obligatory "Japanese bastard!" and proceeded to beat me up. He didn't stop until my mouth was cut and my clothes were spattered with blood. When I got home, my mother asked me what had happened, but I didn't want her to worry, so I just said it was a scuffle with some of the other kids at school. The last thing I wanted was to have her fretting on my account. She was already living in a constant state of fear thanks to the warning from the chairperson of the Democratic Women's Union not to speak any Japanese.

My father, however, seemed quite content with our new life. He never hit my mother. He started working as an agricultural laborer on a cooperative. There weren't any private farms, only cooperatives with teams. He had no choice but to also join the Agricultural Workers' Union and attend compulsory study-meetings twice a week to explore the thoughts of Kim Il-sung and the policies of the Workers' Party.

Everyone in North Korea had to join a group affiliated with the Workers' Party. These groups and unions didn't produce anything. Their sole purpose was to indoctrinate members. Everyone had to understand the words of Kim Il-sung and have a thorough knowledge of party policy.

The big difference between regular workers and farm laborers was that the farm laborers couldn't earn a proper salary. They received a little cash, but their primary form of payment was a share of the harvest every autumn. Distribution was based on man-hours. Every day, your work was assessed. If the amount of work you put in was deemed "standard," you were awarded a count of one man-hour. If the amount of work you put in was deemed "heavy," you were awarded a count of two man-hours.

But when we first arrived? Oh, the party was generosity itself. My father received what was supposed to be a year's supply of rice. Ha!

When we opened the sack, it turned out to contain mostly sweet corn and low-grade cereals.

When I lived in Japan, I never really pondered my life. But after I moved to North Korea, the thing that preoccupied me most was the sheer magnitude of the difference between my old life and my new one. I became obsessed with all the things I had taken for granted before, and all the hardships that marked my life now. But that didn't last long. I soon learned that thought was not free in North Korea. A free thought could get you killed if it slipped out. If you were lucky, you might get sent to some remote mountainous region to do hard labor. Or you might get sent to a concentration camp for political prisoners because you were deemed a "liberal" or a "capitalist" with "bad habits." And bad habits needed to be stamped out. By means of a jackboot to the genitals. Or then again, you might simply be executed.

In the great egalitarian paradise of North Korea, you sure got to know your place quickly. If you were well connected and had friends in the League of Koreans in Japan or in the Korean Workers' Party, you got to live in the capital, Pyongyang, or Wonsan, the country's second-largest city. But if you had no connections, forget it. At the local level, neighbors were clustered into groups of five families each, with a leader who was tasked with reporting everything about the members of the group to the secret police. Even if you were nobody. And being nobody, you were automatically suspect. People like that got sent to remote villages to work as serfs. And by "people like that," I really mean people like us. In North Korea, we were once more the lowest of the low.

We were constantly monitored by the goons of the State Security of North Korea and the secret police. I guess we posed a double threat. We'd brought some dangerous items with us from Japan when we moved—things like bicycles and electrical appliances and half-decent clothes. What if the local villagers came to realize that their standard of living was pitiful? Worse still, what would happen if they got wind of the concept of free thought from us? They might question the wisdom of Kim Il-sung. And that was *verboten*.

We moved to North Korea to escape from our life of poverty in Japan. We didn't see ourselves as taking part in some heroic endeavor to build a future socialist utopia. And now that we were in North Korea? Now what? Well, one thing became clear pretty rapidly. My father's income was nowhere near enough to support a family of six, and we were eating far less well than we had in Japan.

All adults were expected to work. Basically, the ethic was "No work, no dinner." Fine. The only trouble was, the party officials in the village wouldn't give my mother a job since she couldn't speak Korean. She was a very capable woman. She had some technical qualifications, a mathematics certification, and nursing experience, among other things—but none of that made any difference to the party. Eventually, the villagers learned that she was knowledgeable about childbirth, and they would come to her for help with their births. Still they treated her like a third-class citizen, and the party itself continued to view her as worthless. So most days, my mother would simply walk to the mountain behind our house and pick weeds and anything else edible to supplement our diet.

In addition to struggling to find enough food for us, my mother had difficulty cooking it. All she had to work with was a primitive woodstove. The quantity of firewood she could find varied from day to day, so regulating the heat was problematic. The rice she cooked was usually either half-raw or burned. But my father never complained. He always ate her rice with relish. That was the only good thing about moving to North Korea—my father's transformation.

Looking back on it now, the small kindnesses he showed were the least he could do.

My sisters and I were growing fast and always hungry. We were soon fed up with eating nothing but rice. My father sold one of our precious bikes and some of the clothes we'd brought with us to party officials in the village. Armed with a little hard cash at last, he set off for the farmers' market on the outskirts of the village. The state controlled food distribution, and private sales were technically banned. Even so, a blind eye was sometimes turned, and farmers could get away with selling a few vegetables and eggs on the side. As you can imagine, the prices were exorbitant—sometimes ten times higher than the official price.

To our astonishment, my father came back with a pig, a sheep, and a chicken. We decided to keep them in the yard. To my sisters, these animals were like new toys, even though we were raising them for food. I hadn't seen my sisters so excited in a long time.

But that very same afternoon, the village policeman barged into our yard like he owned the place and started poking around. He was a sinister-looking fellow, with hollow cheeks and sunken eyes. I didn't want to look into those terrifying eyes, so I just averted my gaze and concentrated on making the pig feed.

"You stupid Japanese bastard! What are you thinking? Putting rice in the pig feed . . . Rice is for humans, you little shit!"

I was too scared to speak. The rice he was raving about consisted of a few measly grains that had dropped on the floor at lunchtime. I knew I couldn't simply throw them away, so I'd picked them up grain by grain and added them to the pig feed. And now I was being accused of profligacy.

My father burst out of the house, grabbed the policeman by the collar, and decked him. The Tiger of the black market had returned. But not for long. When the policeman finally got back on his feet, he pulled out his gun, wild-eyed. My father stepped back. "Okay, okay.

I got the message. No need to shoot me." The policeman shoved his gun in my father's back and barked at him to march toward the police station. My father looked back at me. "Don't worry!" he cried out as he walked away.

My mother and I feared the worst as we waited and waited for his return. When he finally staggered in around midnight, he couldn't walk properly, and his face was bloody and grotesquely swollen. I hadn't ever liked my father or felt much sympathy for him, but a new feeling stirred inside me that night.

"You have to be careful. All of you. Christ, those fuckers deceived me. The fucking League of Koreans!" he raved. He was shaking, and not just with anger. I could tell something in him had been broken. He was terrified.

I'd never seen him frightened by anything before. When we lived in Japan, if anyone crossed him, he'd simply punch their lights out. Even when he was arrested, he didn't care. But now he was scared, plain and simple. And that scared me to death. When I saw the terror in his eyes and heard the miserable realization in his voice, I knew once and for all that we'd been consigned to hell. It made my flesh crawl to think about it. My father had bought a pig, a chicken, and a sheep to feed his family, and some jealous neighbor had seen fit to rat him out for this gross misdemeanor. And that policeman would happily have killed him for it.

I've thought about that moment many times. From that night on—newly aware of where I was and where the League and the Japanese government had landed me—I studied like mad to make up for my "hostile" background. I naively thought I could overcome it with work and diligence, and was determined to do my utmost to turn things around for my family. My Korean language skills gradually improved, and I was eventually able to speak Korean easily with my father. As I made this progress, I felt myself growing slowly closer to him.

After a year in North Korea, I was in the third year of junior high, and my efforts at school were finally recognized. I became the class monitor. I guess I just wanted to be accepted and prove that I was more than a "Japanese bastard." If one of my classmates got sick and had to be absent from school, I brought him medicine and taught him the things he'd missed in class. I saw it as my duty and responsibility.

But what were we learning? Our lessons went well beyond the standard subjects of spelling, math, and physics. We also had to learn about the miraculous revolutionary changes the divine Kim Il-sung had brought about. The most important thing was how faithful you were to the Great Leader. Teachers and every other adult I knew tried to brainwash us into becoming slavish members of their pseudo-religious cult. I played along. I learned quickly that in that sort of situation, if you want to survive, you have to stifle your critical faculties and just get on with things. I had to pick my battles carefully and not let myself get riled up by every little thing. But the trouble is that some people really do end up brainwashed. They come to believe all the bullshit. But, thankfully, there are also many who don't. And one day, they'll be the downfall of the house of cards that is North Korea.

When I was fourteen years old, I joined the Democratic Youth League. I also became a member of the school committee. I was sick and tired of being told, "You're Japanese, you stupid bastard, so of course you're useless." I knew I wasn't useless, and I was determined to prove it.

At the joining ceremony for the youth groups, you had to stand in front of a bunch of party officials and sing a song in praise of Kim Il-sung. Then you lined up and swore allegiance to him and vowed to do your best to promote his brand of socialism. Then an official tied a red scarf around your neck and pinned a badge on you. The red stood for the blood of the revolution and the spirit of communism.

The Youth League members ranged from fourteen to thirty years old. The lofty aim was to bring about the total victory of socialism. I didn't give a whit about socialism, of course. I just wanted to improve my life and that of my family. Some groups only wore red scarves, but those of us in the Youth League carried membership cards.

I'll never forget the day I received my card. It read, "All of you must protect the foundations of socialism and strive for the triumph of the revolution." The leadership still churns out such vacuous exhortations to this day. Though normally I didn't believe any of that nonsense, even I was kind of taken in for a moment.

I stared and stared at that card, feeling as if perhaps I actually was a person with a noble aim.

That spring, the Youth League spent a month planting rice seedlings and fertilizing them. Planting rice seedlings in the spring was the hardest job, and everyone hated it. It was the first job I was ordered to do. To this day, I can recall every detail of planting those seedlings. I was quite excited to get the task under way, as I'd never planted rice before. I rolled my trousers up to my knees and sank my feet in the cool, watery mud of the paddy field. We formed a line, seedlings at our sides. Our instructor stood on a path between the paddy fields. When he saw that we were ready, he barked, "Go!" as though announcing the start of a race. We leaped into action.

The instructor scrutinized us for a while.

"No!" he barked. "You aren't doing it correctly. Narrow the distance between the seedlings!"

I glanced over my shoulder. And there he was, strutting about self-importantly and shouting orders. I couldn't understand why he was telling us to plant the seedlings closer together. Or why he wasn't doing some of the work himself.

I turned to a classmate laboring next to me.

"What's he talking about?" I asked.

My classmate looked at me as if I were an idiot.

"Don't you *know*?" he asked with a great show of incredulity. "This is the latest scientific method. It can produce more."

I hadn't planted rice seedlings before, but I knew what every Japanese kid learned in elementary school. If you plant rice seedlings too close together, they crowd one another out and can't produce a decent crop. Rice Growing 101, if you like. But then I thought, *This guy can't be an amateur. He must know something I don't. Maybe they've discovered something new.* So I carried on. Needless to say, the crop was a miserable failure. I often wonder how many people starved as a result of that idiotic policy.

At first, I enjoyed the planting. Despite my misgivings, it was a kind of novelty. But after a few hours, I got cramped and sore. I straightened up to stretch my aching back.

"Don't take a rest!" someone snapped at me.

I looked around. It was one of the permanent farmworkers, who was standing there doing nothing at all. I couldn't help myself. "You don't seem to know anything about farming. What gives you the right to boss me around like that?" I mumbled.

I checked to see whether any of the party officials were watching me. They weren't, so I wandered off for a smoke.

After that, I noticed that the permanent farmworkers did hardly any work at all. They spent all their time telling the members of the Youth League and the soldiers what to do. But at the end of the day, the farmers claimed they'd put in a full day's work, and the officials logged their hours without question. We didn't protest. When you find yourself caught in a crazy system dreamed up by dangerous lunatics, you just do what you're told.

Though I kept my mouth shut, I couldn't help but wonder why the farmers were so blatantly two-faced. When listening to the bogus agricultural "experts," they were embarrassingly humble and self-deprecating. But when speaking to us, they turned into tyrants. The reason for this became obvious later that year, at harvest time.

Harvest was known as the "autumn battle." I don't know who came up with that expression, but it has the stamp of Kim Il-sung all over it. Everything was a "battle" or a "march" or a "war." Stirring words to encourage the people to fight hard. And always uttered with that overblown intonation that sounded simultaneously preposterous and deranged.

Come harvest time, we were instructed to line up in the fields just as we had in the spring. Some clown shouted, "Go!" and we moved off together, reaping the rice with our sickles. Sure enough, the instructors were busy barking orders, the full-time farmers pretended to work, and the only people doing any real work at all were the members of the Youth League. It was backbreaking work.

As the sun began to set, I felt a surge of relief at the thought that our workday was nearly over. Except it wasn't. As the evening grew dark, one of the instructors told us to line up old tires on the path that ran between the rice fields. I had no idea who'd brought the tires and placed them there, but we lined them up as instructed.

"What's with the tires?" I asked one of the farmers.

"We have to finish the harvest today," he answered quietly. "Orders from the top."

As night fell, the farmers set fire to the old tires. The light from the stinking flames would enable us to work all night.

Why not go to bed and resume the harvest the next day? The rice wasn't going anywhere in the next six hours. What was the big hurry? The answer was simple: bureaucracy.

The village farms were administered by local "instruction committees." These committees were in charge of everything—machinery, irrigation, materials. Farmers had no choice but to follow the committee's instructions. The system was known as the "feasibility concept."

Feasibility concept! That's what happens to language in countries like North Korea. A totalitarian dictatorship is a "democratic republic." Bondage is known as "emancipation."

But back to the "feasibility concept." Bureaucrats in charge of farm production paid no attention to location whatsoever. North, south, east, west—it made no difference. They couldn't have cared less about the unique features of a particular area. Rigidly uniform agricultural policies were passed off as universal truths. They completely ignored any local environmental conditions and issued the same order to everyone. "Finish planting the rice seedlings by such and such a date!" "This is the deadline for the harvest!" No matter how bizarre the directive, farmers had to keep to the schedule. And so sometimes we worked all night.

If a farmer had the audacity to object to the absurdity of some directive, he was told, "The reason you can't get the job done on time is your total lack of loyalty to Kim Il-sung and the party." And everyone knew what that would mean. So no one dared to complain.

Soldiers and members of the Youth League were sent to work on farms just twice a year, but the real farmers had to work under these ridiculous conditions all the time. They knew that, however long they worked and however much effort they put in, they wouldn't be rewarded for their labors; their pay would be the same. And they had to follow the instructions of amateurs who didn't know what they were talking about. So of course they lost all motivation. Who could blame them?

Working on the farm was physically tough, but I was a teenager at the time, so I could cope with it. The thing I hated most about the work was that I couldn't take a bath or shower at the end of the day. I'd come home caked in mud and smelly with sweat, and all I wanted was to wash it all away. But our house didn't have a bathtub. Nobody's house did. In 1960. In paradise on earth.

In the end, we cobbled together our own makeshift bathtub and tried to make the best of it. I imagine other "returnees" did the same thing. But did they sit in their jerry-rigged tubs, as I did, reminiscing about the past? I remembered the funny washtub of my childhood; I remembered gazing up at the clouds and dreaming of a future of untold possibilities. Instead, here I was, gazing out on hell. I guess I should have wept at the sadness of my plight. But I didn't. Even back then, I was past weeping.

Our ramshackle bath drove our neighbors wild. To them, it was a symbol of Japanese decadence. Bathing was an act of bourgeois self-indulgence; so was changing our clothes every day. Our older neighbors accused us of acting "like landlords." At first, I didn't understand what they meant, but I gathered from their hateful looks that they were referring to some long-lost upper class.

The people around me hardly ever seemed to change or wash their clothes. They hardly ever showered or cleaned themselves. The dirt was ingrained on their bodies, and they were filthy.

From time to time, a hygiene outfit carried out a lice check at school. If you were dirty, you got told off for poor hygiene. But if you admitted you bathed frequently, you were equally told off, in this case for "Japanese decadence." As usual, you couldn't win.

I couldn't let the matter go and said to one of my friends, "They told us to keep ourselves clean, right? If they mean it, then they should be encouraging us to bathe every day."

"What are you talking about? A bath every day? Only a Japanese bastard could advocate something like that," he replied, as though I'd proposed something insane.

I was shocked. Not by his opinion so much as his tone. I'd thought he was my friend. How could he call me a "Japanese bastard" to my face?

Looking back on it, I don't think people even realized it was an offensive term. To them, calling Japanese people bastards was just a statement of fact. North Koreans had been indoctrinated to think that all Japanese were cruel. And to be fair, I tended to call North Koreans "natives." Most of the returnees did the same.

When we weren't working on farms, the Youth League had other jobs, like collecting any resources that could be reused—scrap iron, rubber, empty cans, used paper, and the like. Sometimes we were instructed to search for scrap that could be used in tank or aircraft production. Our teachers would go on about the latest "tank production drive" or "aircraft production drive." Targets were set every month for the number of pounds we had to collect.

But in North Korea, no one threw away anything of value or use. So it was impossible to meet the targets they'd set for us. Even so, if you failed to meet them—as you inevitably did time and again—you were severely reprimanded. As were your parents.

Although this may sound strange, the hardest things for me to collect were the required two rabbit pelts a year. These were used for making hats, earmuffs, and gloves to protect soldiers from the bitter cold. Kids were encouraged to keep rabbits and scavenge food for them on their way to school. This was nothing short of ludicrous, since our chances of catching a rabbit were incredibly remote. And anyone who did manage to trap a rabbit ate it immediately and then sold its skin at the farmers' market. So, what did students do if they couldn't catch rabbits? They had to go to the market and buy a skin. But one skin cost four or five won, a staggering amount when you considered that an average worker's annual salary was only seventy or eighty won.

Needless to say, the teachers scolded any students who couldn't come up with the requisite two pelts. How I remember their hectoring remarks: "If you *can't* get rabbit skins, get some *cement*! If you *can't* get cement, get some *bricks*!"

Cement and bricks were of course valuable as construction materials. If teachers could present a decent quantity of cement and a sufficient number of bricks to high-ranking party members, they would be

40

in the officials' good graces. So they piled pressure on their students to come up with the goods.

Parents of students who struggled in school gave teachers cigarettes or alcohol as a bribe. But the bribes were never enough. The teachers aggressively pressed for more and more. Students who couldn't offer any further bribes didn't want to go to school.

In winter, we were also tasked with gathering a set quota of firewood and charcoal. Some families didn't bother with collecting wood and simply came up with alternative solutions. They made their own peat or even contrived to steal electricity for cooking purposes. Those kids had no way of meeting their targets. As a result, they'd run around the village the night before the deadline, stealing whatever firewood and charcoal they could lay their hands on.

Once beyond school age, individuals were all expected to carry out two functions: to contribute to production and to take part in military operations. The whole system was based on the "Four Military Lines." The key tenets were "arm the entire people," "fortify the entire nation," "build a nation of military leaders," and "complete military modernization." So various militias were formed.

When I grew too old for the Youth League, I had no choice but to join one of these militias. In my case, it was the Laborers' and Farmers' Red Army. I enlisted when I graduated from high school and embarked on a period of training.

The training was professional enough. We learned how to dig trenches and fight to protect our position. We were well trained as snipers. Groups of individuals who were used to working together were formed into military units. The idea was that, in the event of a crisis, the units could be mobilized very quickly. We had exercises twice a year, at the hottest and the coldest time of year. We'd do things like climb a mountain or dig trenches out of the frozen ground. Right from the start, the one thing I kept asking myself was this: What was with the party's obsession with militarizing the entire nation?

At the end of a particularly grueling training period, I said to my closest friend, "Jesus! I can't do this anymore. It's just too hard!" If a member of the secret police had overheard even this petty gripe, I'd have been sent to a concentration camp at once. I wasn't the only one who complained, but it was dangerous to do so.

It was difficult for me to understand why no one ever seemed to question the point of the training, but I had to remember that they'd been brainwashed since they were babes by one or another barking, hysterical voice. When they were kids, it came from their teachers; later, it came from party officials, who drilled the same messages into them day after day after day. "The dictator of South Korea started the Korean War! He was a pro-American imperialist! The leader of a puppet government! A poodle!" As a result, the militarization of the nation was entirely justified in their eyes. They were the only bulwark against imperialist American or South Korean attacks. And anyone who doubted or questioned this wisdom must have been a counter-revolutionary. A subversive. A traitor.

As you question whether they could really have been so completely brainwashed, keep in mind that North Koreans had never experienced a liberal democracy. They had no concept of what it was or what it meant. My comrades had only ever known or heard of colonial rule at the hands of Japan and dictatorship at the hands of Kim Il-sung. And before that was the miserable feudal period of the Korean dynasties. They'd only ever known bondage. North Koreans didn't have anything to compare their country with because they'd never experienced anything else. Even when Kim Il-sung did something particularly brutal or horrific, no one raised an eyebrow. "Remember the time of Japanese colonial rule!" "Never forget the cruelty of American imperialism!"

Without any other information at their disposal, young North Koreans simply fell for the propaganda.

April 1964. It was our fourth year in North Korea. It was freezing cold. If you're thinking that April should have meant the onset of spring, forget it. The snow outside came up to my waist. April 15, 1964, was Kim Il-sung's birthday, therefore one of the year's biggest holidays. That particular year, it was a total catastrophe for my family.

Everyone in North Korea celebrated that wretched day. Every family received two and a half pounds of pork and some sweets and fruit—unheard-of luxuries at any other time of year. Amazingly, people were duped by these "gifts"; they really thought Kim Il-sung cared for them. I never fell for the ploy, but my sisters and I nonetheless still looked forward to the occasion as much as everyone else. Pork and sweets and fruit all in one day? It was the only day of the year when I wasn't hungry. What was not to like?

During our first years there, my father used to go out on the eve of the great celebration to sell a few household goods we'd brought from Japan so that he could buy some meat and alcohol. And, lo and behold, when the great day came, our neighbors would suddenly appear out of nowhere to pay a visit to my mother—whom they usually ignored unless they needed her help with the delivery of a baby. On the Great Leader's birthday, they were all smiles.

People came to our house from far and wide. Party and military bigwigs, some guy known as the "combat commander," the village headman, and various hangers-on all made an appearance. Though our house was in the depths of the mountains, they somehow all managed to get there. They were no fools. They knew we had delicious food and drink to share. They knew that our crummy Japanese house was—shock and horror—clean. And, perhaps most important, they knew that there was an abundance of alcohol to be had.

That year, 1964, my mother and I made a fire in the kitchen, and she cooked for hours. All the hypocrites and parasites arrived and had a grand old time enjoying the fruits of her labor. Everyone got drunk and laughed and sang until one or two o'clock in the morning. Eventually, everyone filed out, except for a barber named Han Ju-han, who was so wasted, he couldn't stand up. Bizarre as it may sound, barbers were something of a rarity in North Korea at the time, so he was favored by various higher-ups. Though we asked him to stay overnight, he insisted on going home, finally managing to stand up and stumble out into the dark. There were no streetlamps, and he didn't have a flashlight. And there was an unbelievable amount of snow. He could easily fall into a river or slip off a mountain path. But he insisted on leaving, and my parents, my sisters, and I were so tired that we went to bed as soon as he left.

I woke up feeling unbearably hot. When I opened my eyes, flames were licking the ceiling. At first, I thought I must be dreaming. Then I leaped from my bed and screamed at everyone to get up. But they were sleeping soundly, their bellies full of good food. I shook my parents and then my sisters, yelling at them to wake up. My heart was racing, and I was sure we were all going to die. I finally succeeded in waking them, and when they saw what was happening, they jumped up.

We didn't have time to get dressed or bring anything with us. Seconds after we left the burning building, the whole thing collapsed. It really was that narrow an escape. I have nightmares about it to this day.

It turned out that the celebrated barber had caused the fire. Confronted with the impenetrable snow and his inebriation, he'd stumbled back to our house. But instead of coming inside, he staggered to the shed where we kept straw and firewood. He made himself a bed of straw, drunkenly lit a cigarette, and promptly fell asleep. The whole place went up like a tinderbox. Apparently, he woke up and tried to shout, but he was too drunk and panicked to do anything more. He was so scared, he just crawled away into the night.

Soon enough, several villagers came out into the street and scrambled to help us try to put it out. Some of them formed a line from the well to the house and passed buckets of water. Others brought water up from the paddy field in whatever containers they could find. Some even tried to use snow. But their efforts were futile. Our house was completely incinerated. Along with everything we owned. Just like that, we became homeless. Just when I thought things couldn't get any harder, everything collapsed around us. I couldn't help but feel we were cursed.

The following morning, my father and I went to see some of the very officials who'd enjoyed our hospitality the day before and asked if the party could help us out. Less than twenty-four hours earlier, they'd happily eaten our food and gotten drunk on the alcohol my father had bought. Now they totally changed their tune. "What are you talking about, you Japanese bastard? Why should we house *you*? However, we will grant you special dispensation to cut down some trees so that you can build a new house for your family. That is the party's pronouncement," they said, clearly pleased about what they considered to be a great act of generosity. Their hypocrisy made me sick.

We went straight to the foreman of the maintenance division to borrow an oxcart. My mother retrieved some rice and the woodstove from the wreckage of our burned-out house and made two big rice balls for us. My father and I trudged off to the forest, which was about five miles from the village. A policeman told us where we could cut down some trees, and we quickly got to work. After felling twelve trees, we took a lunch break.

"Eat both rice balls," my father said to me.

I felt very awkward as I tried to hand one rice ball back. I was not used to him being kind or thoughtful.

"No, no, no," I said. "Let's share them."

But he pushed me away. I lost my balance and fell. The rice balls slipped from my hands and careened down the slope. My father chased after them and retrieved them. They were covered with mud, but my father handed them to me anyway. "Your mother made them for you, so just eat them!" he said. And to my amazement, he burst into tears. I'd never seen him cry or show much emotion. So of course I started blubbering too. Somehow, my father showing his feelings made everything seem that much worse. But I sure forced down those rice balls. And that small kernel of love for my father, planted when we first arrived, began to grow.

There was one person in the village who was kind to us. His name was Mr. Chon, and he was a smith. He tried to cheer up my mother, who had hit rock bottom. Whenever we thanked him for a bit of extra food that he had scrounged for us or expressed our gratitude to him for stopping by to check on us, he just said, "Hey, next time, you'll be the ones helping *me* out!" But most of the villagers ignored us; some even seemed glad that our house had been destroyed. They'd been jealous of us ever since we'd arrived, and they now clearly felt vindicated. "Oh! Why do those la-di-da Japanese bastards get to live in a better house than we do? How come returnees get to live in such a nice house?" Our shack of a house was no better than theirs, of course. It just had a tile roof. But that was enough to invoke their anger. They said the same thing about our Japanese clothes. They were cheap and increasingly tattered and not remotely fashionable, but to the locals, they were luxury items. While we were clearing up our burned-out wreck of a house, some villagers walked past and openly sneered at us. I couldn't help but notice that they were the very same people who'd wolfed down my mother's dishes and guzzled my father's booze just days before. That's when I started calling them "natives."

When we got to work building our new house, Mr. Chon was the only villager who helped us. First, we took the trees we'd cut down in the forest to a sawmill for processing. Then we laid down the foundations using stones we'd gathered by the river. My mother and sisters dug mud that would be used for the walls. A few weeks later, we thatched a straw roof to keep the rain out. Though we felt some relief when the house was complete, we still had no household goods or food or clothes. My father had to spend most of our meager household budget to procure some basic foodstuffs from the farmers' market. We didn't have enough money for clothes, so we each had just two outfits, and were forced to go without underwear.

Through it all, my mother said over and over again, "I'm so sorry! I'm so sorry!"

"I'm sorry too. I always make your life so hard," my father said. Again, I was shocked by his words. He seemed to have become a different man. I felt conflicted. It was the first time I'd seen my father look after my mother, which was obviously a welcome development. But at the same time, I thought, *Is this what it takes to get my father to care for my mother? Total ruination?* Seemed he'd taken an awfully long time to get there.

Even now, I sometimes wonder why my father was so different in North Korea from the man he'd been in Japan. I used to think it was related to his physical strength. In Japan, that was the thing that had given him real power. But in North Korea, his strength was meaningless. In fact, it was more of a liability than an asset. But I think the issue was more complicated than that. In Japan, he faced endless bigotry, prejudice, and discrimination. The only way he could express his feelings and fight back was through violence. But back then, as he saw it, he was fighting to defend his Korean brothers.

After we moved into the creaky shack we'd built, my father gradually started talking more about his past.

He kept mulling over the same old resentments. And who could blame him? "It's incredible. I really tried to fight for my compatriots in Japan. I'd have died for them. And what was my reward?" Then he'd gesture at our surroundings. "This!"

Sometimes, he couldn't contain his anger and frustration. "I can't believe the way those people deceived me! Masaji, if you ever get back to Japan, tell them what I think of them!"

Oddly enough, I never heard him complain about or blame the political system of North Korea. I finally realized that he'd never experienced true freedom. He'd been born under Japanese colonial rule and then shipped off to a life of slave labor. So he'd never known anything else. That might explain why he seemed to grow milder and more accepting over time.

My mother, however, became more frightened by the day.

Soon after we moved into our rickety shack, a young police officer came by. According to this fellow, our family register was defective. My mother's nationality had been recorded as Japanese, and her name had been recorded as Miyoko Ishikawa.

"You must change your name!" he shouted, glaring at my mother.

"She's Japanese," I said. "She doesn't need to change her name."

"You're living in North Korea. You must change your name!" he cried, bellowing into her face. "You must use a North Korean name!"

"Don't you touch her!" I said, running over to defend her. "If you so much as lay a finger on her, I'll kill you!"

He seemed to wilt a little at that.

My mother couldn't understand a word he was saying, but even so, she looked very scared.

The police officer threw back his shoulders and stuck out his chest in a totally unconvincing attempt to look big.

"Well," he blustered, "change your name . . . for *next time*!"

Whatever that meant.

And with that, he stomped out of the house.

I turned to my mother and told her not to worry about it. I didn't want to say more for fear of worrying her.

She sighed and pulled on her frayed rucksack. She looked so frail and weary, as if she lacked the energy anymore to even be afraid.

"I need to go forage for food for dinner."

And with that, she plodded wearily up the mountain to search for bracken, ferns, wild mushrooms—anything remotely edible. She wore baggy work pants covered with patches and ragged shoes. I wanted to cry like she sometimes did. She often broke down and sobbed for hours at a time. I tried to console her, but I could never find the words. They didn't exist.

When I was in high school, I really believed that if I only studied hard enough, I could find a way out of my situation and save my family. Despite the house-fire catastrophe and the discrimination we faced every day, I was genuinely convinced that if I put in enough effort, I could escape this awful predicament and find a way forward into a better life for myself and my family. As graduation approached, I studied harder than ever.

One day, three months before graduation, the teacher handed out a form. We had to fill in what we wanted to do after graduation and describe our future dreams. It was a cruel exercise since we had no real choice in the matter. But I didn't know that yet. Physics was my best subject, and I wanted to study physics at university and then become a researcher. I wrote dutifully:

I want to go to university and study physics.

Someone asked me what I'd written, so I told him. Some of my classmates overheard what I said and started laughing at me.

"Ha! This guy wants to go to university," a classmate said.

More people started laughing. I couldn't understand it, so as you can imagine, I lost my temper. "Yeah. I want to go to university. What is wrong with that?" I said.

I found out the next day during my counseling session, which was kindly offered by the school principal and my class teacher. This "academic and career counseling" turned out to be a total joke. I learned that after high school graduation in North Korea, there were three paths to choose from. Except there weren't. In reality, your path was chosen for you. Basically, if you were clever and your birth and background were good enough, you were sent to university. If you were physically strong, you went to the military academy or became a common soldier. The rest were sent to workplaces as laborers. The most important factor in path determination was not how hard you worked but your assigned caste.

The three castes were "nucleus" (or "core"), "basic" (or "wavering"), and "hostile." Three criteria determined your caste: your birth and background, your perceived loyalty to the party, and your connections. Academic achievements had nothing to do with it, no matter how excellent they were. Your whole life was determined by which caste you'd been consigned to. If you were deemed "core," a rosy future awaited you. But if you were deemed "hostile," you were the lowest of the low and would remain so for life. No career path. No chance of bettering yourself. No way out.

It turned out the school principal was just another party apparatchik. On that particular day, his job was to inform me of which caste I'd been consigned to. I was told that I'd been deemed "hostile." And that was that.

My head was spinning. I felt like I was about to sink through the floor, as if I were plunging into an abyss. Questions jostled for position in my mind. Deemed? By whom? What for? Hadn't I studied hard? Hadn't I worked hard for the party? Had it all been a waste of time and effort? What was going to happen to my family now?

I'd known that North Korea was no "paradise on earth" ever since I set foot in the place. But I'd thought that going to university was my one chance to better my position. After all, back in Japan, that had been one of the enticements to move to North Korea. They'd *promised* that we would get a good education for free. It was a huge incentive. But also a complete, barefaced lie. It's difficult to put into words what this discovery did to me. I was totally and utterly shattered. The realization that I was consigned to spend the rest of my life at the very bottom of society with no chance of escape came crashing down on my head like an avalanche. I lost all hope for the future, and I felt like a part of me died that day.

The following day, some documents arrived from the People's Committee Bureau of Labor. Knowing that no amount of effort or work would make any difference to my future, I didn't care what kind of job I would get. With one exception. If you were a farmer, there was no hope of promotion—and no chance of ever escaping the village. Like my father. So when it came time to fill in the part of the form where you had to say what kind of job you hoped to do, I wrote:

factory work

In reality, it didn't matter what you wrote. So even my pathetic "wish" to work in a factory was denied, and I was assigned to work on the village farm. When the instructor from the local People's Committee came to announce my workplace, my dissatisfaction must have been clear, because he suddenly snapped at me, "The son of a farmer must be a farmer. That's the way it is in this country. You should be grateful that you and the likes of your family get any work at all."

And then, by way of consolation, he told me that farming wasn't the worst job. It was, after all, better than working in the coal mine. And people like us—those of us who'd come over from Japan, the lowest of the low—should thank our lucky stars.

I knew of course that the party was hostile toward us, but I hadn't realized until that moment that it was a deliberate policy to send Japanese people to the very bottom of society. I was stunned that this guy would openly admit such a thing.

Suddenly, I felt completely overwhelmed. By rage. Frustration. Despair. And all I could do was walk off in the direction of the mountain and weep. Someone once said, "If a crying baby could tear down the universe, it would." That's how I felt that day. I wanted to demolish the whole universe, but the sad truth was, it had already come crashing down around my head.

I couldn't scream and cry and vent my despair at home because my mother would hear me, and she was already at the end of her tether. I couldn't bear to cause her any more suffering. I also wasn't sure how to talk to my sisters about how I felt. I didn't want to break them too. So at home I kept quiet and silently cursed my fate. I knew then I was destined for a life of hell on earth, and there was absolutely nothing I could do about it.

Before starting my new job, I tried to take a philosophical approach to the prospect of farmwork. I told myself that farmers work hard all over the world. It's a tough life full of grueling days, but it has a kind of dignity to it. A nobility, even. No. That's not the right word. It has a certain grandeur to it. Even when I was called up to do farmwork back in my days at elementary school, I always felt that I was contributing in some small way to a much larger endeavor. Farming consisted of many small parts—each of them laborious enough, no doubt—but each one required its own set of skills and a kind of wisdom.

It was a nice thought. As soon as I started working full-time on the farm, I was reminded of the North Korean way of farming that I'd witnessed back in my Youth League days. It was staggeringly crude and idiotic. As usual, the party barked out its policy in a fatuous, hysterical slogan: "Plant rice all over the country! Harvest all over the country!" To this day, I cringe at the memory of those words.

When I was a kid, I sometimes used to watch farmers at work in Japan. Even at the time, it struck me that growing crops was a bit like raising children. The farmers cherished and nurtured their crops, treating them with love and care. In North Korea, our instructors said the Japanese system was hopelessly inefficient. "Our country uses *Juche* farming. You must tame the land and become its master. That is the only way to cultivate large quantities of crops!" The *Juche* farming model essentially treated rice farming like factory mass production. Centuries of rice-planting techniques were treated with total contempt. We were ordered to shove them closer together, to plant more, to plant faster, to churn out as much as possible. The farmers knew better but had no choice but to do what they were told—and no motivation to try to do better.

By the time I started farming, all this nonsense had been going on for some time. The party members must have realized that things were not going well, because they had begun allowing farming families to form groups and take out leases on small plots of land. The idea was to increase farmers' motivation. But they bungled it yet again. It didn't matter how much effort you put into your independent plot or how much food you actually produced, because the party simply took it. No matter how carefully you'd tended your crop, your overall annual allocation remained the same. What kind of motivation does that provide?

Meanwhile, so-called farming experts kept barking at us to mechanize our farming techniques and use new fertilizing chemicals. But we had no equipment for mechanization. And there were no chemicals. We were being ordered to do the impossible.

Maddeningly, I couldn't even go straight home after work. I had to log my daily production total before I left. And then, twice a week, I had to attend a kind of ideological study meeting no matter how exhausted I was. Week after week, we were inundated with the thoughts of Kim Il-sung, the heroic history of the Korean Workers' Party, or earnest analysis of some ridiculous party newspaper article. And *after* the meeting, we were forced to stay for further discussions and presentations that always boiled down to the same thing: the brilliance of Kim Il-sung's political philosophy. So there we were, pretending to take an interest in our Fearless Leader's latest musings, until about ten o'clock at night, hungry and exhausted. I suppose you could call it brainwashing of sorts, but to be honest, we were all too tired to pay much attention. It was just more propaganda and hot air. But if we were foolish enough to miss a study meeting, we were suspected of being dissidents and put under surveillance by the secret police. As if all that weren't enough, we also had to endure the time-wasting farce of our Laborers' and Farmers' Red Army training twice a year. In the end, all that mattered was whether our loyalty toward Kim Il-sung appeared credible. So we became masters at faking it. Everyone did. To do anything else could have gotten us killed.

Everywhere we heard the endless drip drip drip of that wretched word *Juche*. "Our *Juche* farming method . . . the revolutionary *Juche* approach to production . . ." It was always the *Juche* something or other. Everybody nodded, but no one ever seemed to question what the word actually meant.

The word could be translated in a number of ways. It could mean self-reliance, autonomy, independence, or responsibility—all the things we weren't allowed to have. According to the *Juche* "philosophy," "human beings are the masters of the world, so they get to decide everything." It suggested we could reorganize the world, hew out a career for ourselves, and be the masters of our destiny. This was laughable, of course, but that's always the way with totalitarian regimes. Language gets turned on its head. Serfdom is freedom. Repression is liberation. A police state is a democratic republic. And we were "the masters of our destiny." And if we begged to differ, we were dead.

Even as people faced incredible hardship and deprivation of both the physical and mental variety and wasted away under food shortages, we weren't allowed to think for ourselves or take any initiative. The penalty for thinking was death. I can never forgive Kim Il-sung for taking away our right to think.

After a few months, I asked to be transferred to the "machinery division," which was about to get hold of three Russian tractors. Tractor drivers' man-hours counted double, so naturally, everyone wanted to be a tractor driver. I was hardly surprised when I encountered the usual prejudice when I first applied.

"You do realize that tractors can be driven on the roads?"

"Erm, yes."

"And you realize that roads in this country are classified as military secrets?"

Huh?

Bizarrely, that was the truth. At the time, all railroads, roads, and rivers were military secrets. You revealed their locations at peril of death.

"Doesn't it occur to you that someone like you shouldn't have access to that information?"

Someone like me. A Japanese traitor in the making. But I refused to accept yet another rejection, so I wrote to the People's Committee in the village.

As you know,

I wrote with mock indignation,

I've worked hard to build the great socialist future of the motherland. And now I want to work harder still. So I wish to be a tractor driver. I appreciate that tractors have to travel long distances, and I'll never remember the route from one journey to the next, but I'll do my best.

To my astonishment, my application was accepted. I received a few driving lessons and passed the tractor-driving test on the first attempt. Things seemed to be finally looking up.

Around the same time, my father was suddenly transferred from the farm to some sort of fruit-producing cooperative. No one knew why. But he continued to work his backside off. We both did. But no matter how hard we worked, we couldn't make enough to support our family. My sisters were still in school, and I'll never forget how lousy we felt about not being able to support them properly. I can't even describe the hopelessness and despair I felt walking into my house in Dong Chong-ri after a long day of work and facing their hunger. It didn't matter what we did—there was simply never enough food to go around.

In theory, if you were able-bodied, you got seven hundred grams of food a day. The elderly and sick got three hundred grams a day. That's right. If you were sick or old, you were penalized. But the reality was even worse. The reality was "no work, no dinner." So old people had to work until they died. They truly did.

My mother still wasn't allowed to work. She still went to the mountain every day to pick mushrooms and weeds. We ate some, and she sold the rest on the black market. The secret police clamped down from time to time, and there was always a guy on the lookout for them. Whenever he yelled, "Police!" the market traders instantly vanished. They occasionally managed to bribe the police to leave them be, but you had to be smart, because the police would double-cross you without compunction.

We could just barely survive; it was hand to mouth. But somehow, I still thought I could miraculously find a better job. Even so, I have to admit that I enjoyed driving the tractor. We lived under constant surveillance so stifling you couldn't breathe. But on the tractor, I was strangely free. It was one of the only times I was entirely in my own world, and I could survey things, unobserved. I can't tell you what pleasure that gave me.

People ridiculed me. "What on earth are you doing?" they asked. "Why are you working so hard?" They didn't understand that driving that tractor was the only freedom I had, my only respite from the orders and insults that assaulted us day in and day out. So no, I wasn't crazy. Work was my only refuge.

And I just enjoyed driving that tractor.

CHAPTER 3

There's a saying, "Sadness and gladness follow each other." As I see it, people who experience equal amounts of sadness and happiness in their lives must be incredibly blessed. Some people lead a painful life full of nothing but sorrow. I should know.

I became a tractor driver in the summer of 1966. Soon thereafter, a letter arrived via the Red Cross from my mother's brother in Japan. By the time we received it, it was dog-eared and the ink had run in some places. My mother had sent her relatives several letters over the years, but she'd never gotten any response.

When this letter finally came, my mother opened it with great excitement. She read it silently and quickly. But when she came to the second page, the letter fell out of her hands and she collapsed on the floor.

"Mom! What's wrong? What happened?" I asked, running over to her.

I picked up the letter and saw that it contained news of her mother's death:

Your mother was calling your name until she passed away.

I recalled my grandmother's last words to me. "You're Japanese," she'd said. I remember how sad her eyes were. She knew her history. She understood what awful things go on under colonial rule. I knew that my grandmother had tried desperately to change my mother's mind about leaving Japan but to no avail. I still remember looking for her at Shinagawa Station—but she hadn't come to see us off.

After my grandmother's death, my mother's face quickly developed deep wrinkles. She suddenly became more weathered, worn, and frail. These weren't the wrinkles of old age; they were wrinkles of pain. I wanted to make her life easier, but I couldn't see any way of doing that. Whatever effort I made, our food allocation remained the same. Everything remained the same.

And soon enough, more misery arrived . . .

On a nice sunny day in the early spring of 1968, a truck came rumbling into our village. Then another, and another. Suddenly, a military unit raced into the village and came to a stop. One of them, someone who appeared to be the leader, ordered us to gather.

He surveyed us skeptically and declared, "This village will now serve as our garrison."

Then he walked away.

Garrison? A garrison usually describes a fortified place where soldiers are housed when they are sent in to protect an area. But what were we being protected against? Were we about to get invaded? We didn't even know the name of the military unit.

The head of the village rushed up to us and told us that these soldiers were under the direct command of Kim Chan-bon. But we got no more explanation than that. The soldiers were there, protecting our area from God knew what for God knew how long.

I soon discovered that this Kim Chan-bon character and Kim Il-sung had been brothers-in-arms. Kim Chan-bon had become a powerful figure in the party and the author of some major military innovations. Everyone around me kept dwelling on that, but it still didn't explain what he was doing in our village with his merry band of men.

A few days passed. Everyone was on tenterhooks, the tension in the air like electricity. Everyone watched their back and chose their words carefully. One morning as I was about to leave for work, I caught sight of a couple of soldiers approaching our house.

I immediately told my mother and sisters to hide inside, and then I blocked the front door to stop them. A scary-looking soldier came up to me.

"Pack up your things and get out of here immediately!" he said.

"Why? Could you please explain?" I asked.

My heart was pounding and my blood was boiling, but I tried to appear calm.

"Why?" he barked. "You ask me why? Your *songbun*, of course. Surely you know you're a 'hostile,' the lowest of the low. Now fuck off!"

And with that, he turned and stomped off with the other soldier standing nearby. And just like that, they were gone.

We weren't alone. Several other families were also told to leave. According to our orders, we had to move to a village called Pyungyang-ri, several miles away. So we packed up our few belongings and set off. When we got there, there was no house for us. We found shelter in a vacant house that had been built for a farm laborer. We had no idea what had happened to him; he'd probably collapsed and died of exhaustion and despair.

Luckily, I could continue my work as a tractor driver. My father and sisters started working on the local agricultural team. And my mother? She continued to go off into the mountains in search of weeds just as she had before.

Several members of Kim Chan-bon's military unit came to our new village too. Their behavior was positively criminal. They stole animals that the laborers had taken great care of, and killed and ate them. They filched sweet corn and potatoes from the village's food storehouse. They ransacked the farm-equipment factory and made off with motors and power sawmills on their trucks. They seduced young women by promising to marry them, with no intention of doing so, of course. We all loathed and despised them.

The higher party officials in Pyungyang-ri and our old village disappeared. Kim Chan-bon's boys were in control now. It became so bad that we were terrified to go outside even in the middle of the day. Soldiers picked fights with people for no reason and beat them severely.

Our tumbledown house was almost able to keep out the rain, but the wind rattled through the place constantly. It was still the snowy season, and the temperature dropped well below freezing at night. We kept a stove going all night. And thank goodness for the wind since it meant we didn't have to worry about carbon-monoxide poisoning.

There wasn't a mattress to be found, so the six of us just huddled around the stove. First we warmed our backs; then we warmed our stomachs, repeatedly twisting and turning all night. Occasionally, we actually fell asleep for a little while. Because we were always changing positions throughout the night, my father and I often bumped heads. Sometimes we burst out laughing like raving lunatics. If you suffer long enough, it almost becomes funny, and you can find yourself laughing at the most miserable situations. I guess it's a kind of hysteria.

Once I woke up in the middle of the night and discovered that Masako, my youngest sister, was missing. I panicked and dashed out of the house. I saw her footsteps in the snow and followed them all the way back to our old village. Sure enough, there she was, standing in front of our old house, sobbing and sobbing.

As soon as she saw me, she said, "This is our house! I don't want to leave it!"

I hauled her up onto my back and trudged off to Pyungyang-ri under the moonlight. The snow glistened and sparkled, masking the desolation of the scene before me. The cold cut through my tattered clothes, but Masako's weight kept me warm. All her sobbing had tired her out, and she soon fell asleep on my back. I don't think I ever felt as close to her as I did that night. Her desperation, her fear, her exhaustion—all of it seeped through her thin clothes and straight into my heart.

Kim Chan-bon's thugs continued to oppress us and treat all the villagers like their personal slaves. We had to serve them whatever food they demanded—and of course, it was never enough. They always made the same preposterous claims: "We fight for our country! We need more!"

I wanted to reply, "Battle? What battle? There is no battle. What are you talking about? All you do is spread misery and despair and terrorize decent, hardworking people. And how much do you think *we* get to eat? The people who actually *produce* the food while you go around beating people up?"

But of course I kept mum. They'd have killed me if I'd spoken out.

Amazingly, even in these direst of times, I suddenly fell in love. Her name was Rim Su-yon. She was nineteen, and she was the prettiest young woman I'd ever seen. I met her on the farm where she took care of rabbits kept for breeding. I used to deliver grass there on my tractor-driving route. I had never experienced those feelings for anyone before, and I didn't know what to do. Every time I tried to talk to her, she left me tongue-tied, so I just avoided talking to her altogether. But I thought about her constantly.

One day, when I was unloading the grass, she came up and offered to help. We worked in total silence. The following day, she came back and helped me again—and the day after too. One day she finally broke the silence and asked me if I was going to participate in an upcoming soccer competition. I told her I couldn't because I didn't own any shorts. The next time I saw her, she gave me a pair of shorts that she had made out of white nylon. I turned to her and blurted out, "I love you—so will you marry me?" Quite the pickup line.

She looked at me timidly. "Could you get my mother's consent?" she asked. Now I knew she liked me too. I felt my heart swell with hope.

The following day, I gathered my courage and went to her house. Her father had passed away a long time ago, so I told Su-yon's mother that I wanted to marry her. To be fair, she didn't interrupt me or cut me short but heard me out with great tenderness.

Su-yon stood next to her, hanging on my every word. I can picture her even now. She was blushing, and her ears had gone red.

Her mother remained silent for a moment, looking grave. My heart was racing, beating so fast, it felt like it was going to gallop away without me.

"I'm sorry to say . . . a Japanese husband for my daughter . . . well, that wouldn't be acceptable, I'm afraid." She looked as though she felt guilty about her decision. I sensed that she was casting about for an explanation that would somehow assuage me.

"You see, the thing is . . . well, I'm sure you're a perfectly upstanding young man . . . I mean, I know you are. But the thing is . . . if my daughter married a returnee, well, we'd be in a dangerous situation too, you see."

I clenched my fists until they went white. I looked at Su-yon. She had turned pale.

I can't remember exactly what I did after that. I must have run off, ashamed. But I do remember the thoughts that clattered through my mind.

What were you thinking? A man whose quality of life is no better than that of a beggar! Who in their right mind would marry me? It had been laughable to think Su-yon's mother would ever give her consent.

The next time I saw Su-yon at the farm, I wanted to run and hide. But she hugged me and whispered, "I'm sorry. Take me somewhere and let's escape together." How I wanted to run away with her, to live out this fantasy—but where could we possibly go? And what about my poor mother and sisters? I could never abandon them; it was as impossible as my dream of bettering myself or going to college. Soon after, I heard that Su-yon married a bigwig in Pyongyang. I decided not to fall in love with anybody ever again.

A year later, Kim Chan-bon and his cronies suddenly disappeared. I didn't know the official details, but there was a rumor in the village that his unit had been dismissed. There were no mass media in those days, so all news came by word of mouth, but the grapevine was reliable enough most of the time. In the end, it came out that Kim Chan-bon had been purged by Kim Il-sung.

It was the usual story. For a while, Kim Chan-bon had been the apple of the Great Leader's eye. Kim Chan-bon could do no wrong. But he made a sincere effort to modernize and better organize the military. And that proved to be his downfall. It enabled him to build up his own power base within the military and push through his own initiatives. It wasn't long before Kim Chan-bon had amassed power over an entire swathe of North Korea, effectively carving out his own autonomous region. Kim Il-sung obviously saw that as a challenge and a threat. So he was purged.

We returned to Dong Chong-ri right away. Fortunately, our house was still standing. When we arrived, we got some water from the well, boiled it, and drank a toast. I looked at my parents' wizened faces as we drank that toast. My father was fifty-five; my mother was forty-four and had about eight teeth left. What on earth were we drinking a toast to? A better future? A return to the past? I don't know. We were just overjoyed to be out of the Kim Chan-bon nightmare, I guess.

"I want to eat a rice ball coated with sweetened red beans," my mother said after our toast.

My father looked bereft, as my mother never asked for anything. He knew it would be impossible to fulfill even such a modest request. Red beans were as expensive as rice, and sugar was even more dear. A sack cost a hundred won on the black market, a ridiculously huge sum for us.

"Don't worry!" she said, knowing what he must be thinking. "Come to think about it, I couldn't eat a rice ball if I tried. I don't have enough teeth. My rice-ball-eating days are over."

And then she just laughed.

I hadn't heard her laugh for ages. It was contagious. We all began to laugh together—until tears sprang to our eyes.

Three uneventful years passed after Kim Chan-bon's unit was dismissed. We still struggled with the miseries of poverty, of course. But at least our life was peaceful. The only newsworthy event during that time was that my sister Eiko received a marriage proposal at the age of twenty-three, from a man named Kan Ki-son who was originally from Kobe. His father was suffering from late-stage cancer, so he wanted to get married before his old man passed away. His family was wealthy—which was unusual for returnees—so my father thought that his family and our family weren't a good match. He politely turned the proposal down. Even so, Kan's mother started coming to our house to plead her case.

"I want your daughter to be my daughter-in-law," she said. Although she came to ask several times, still my father balked.

Early in 1972, a middle-aged man showed up at our house one day. At first, I thought he was one of Kan's relations. I was really surprised when I took a good look: it was none other than Young Seok-pong, an old friend of my father's who had been a member of the General Association of Korean Residents back in Japan.

He dropped the bag he was carrying and flung his arms around my father's shoulders.

"How have you all been? You've sure grown up a lot!" Young said to us. My mother invited him in.

Then he opened his bag. He handed me a watch and took out some scarves for my sisters. I couldn't believe my eyes. Japanese watches were a coveted rarity. Everybody longed to get ahold of one. He then reached into his bag and pulled out a bottle of alcohol for my father. But that wasn't the end of it. He produced medicine, sugar, and several other valuable commodities and lined them up on the table. My mother burst into tears.

He and my father drank until late into the night. I could hear them talking in hushed tones.

"Look at me!" my father said. "I used to be called 'Tiger,' but now I'm a wreck of a man, thanks to the fucking League of Korean Residents in Japan. Those deceitful bastards!"

"Hey, careful," Young said as he glanced around the room. "Walls have ears, you know! Watch your back!"

My father said nothing but nodded.

"Anyway," Young continued, "let's see if we can help each other out from now on. I gather you've been through a lot of difficulties."

He was vice chairman of the party committee in some city or other and a very busy man, but after that night, he managed to visit us from time to time. As soon as he found out about Eiko's offer of marriage, he paid Kan a visit. "He's a good man. Kind and gentle. Don't worry about the money issue," he said to Eiko. And he recommended that my father reconsider his position. After all, Kan was a returnee too.

That settled it. They fixed a date for the wedding two months later. Sadly, we couldn't get any new clothes or even buy a futon for her. Kan's mother told us that as long as she could get married, that was enough. She didn't need to bring any kind of dowry with her.

But Young gave some money to my mother. "Here. Make her pretty with this," he said.

I was very impressed. Moved, even. His thoughtfulness was like a breath of fresh air. We rarely witnessed or experienced any real humanity or warmth in our daily life. Everyone was always thinking of themselves—how to get ahead, pretending to care about the party, watching their own backs, scrambling for food, and using cigarettes and alcohol as bribes to get in with people who had power. To be fair, it was the only way to survive. The system had dehumanized them completely. Us. The sad thing was that I was starting to think the same way myself. But Young's behavior reminded me what it was to be a human being. And I came to recognize that, no matter how difficult the reality, you mustn't let yourself be beaten. You must have a strong will. You have to summon what you know is right from your innermost depths and follow it.

One day, Mr. Young appeared at our house, looking completely disheveled. Normally he was fastidious, but on this particular day, his hair looked tousled and his eyes were bloodshot. Worst of all, he looked scared to death. He called out my father's name and then grasped his hands silently for a while. Then he started talking madly.

He explained that he'd attended a New Year's party. There were some party bigwigs in attendance, and poor Young had made a slip of the tongue. Apparently, after moving to North Korea, he'd written letters to a man by the name of Ham Do-kusu, chairman of the League of Koreans in Japan. He'd known Ham for years, but he never got a reply. Naturally, Ham's behavior annoyed him.

Young mistakenly brought this up at the party. He said something to the effect of, "Do-kusu only became chairman because everybody helped him and supported him. But he doesn't appreciate what everyone did for him. Now he's far too grand to write back to the likes of me. What a snob!"

That turned out to be a fatal blunder. The following day, Young was removed from his party position. Criticizing Kim Do-suku meant criticizing Kim Il-sung himself.

Young looked a bit calmer after talking to my father.

"Let's live strong, shall we? The future will be better. I know it will. You'll see," my father said. I guess he couldn't think of anything better to say.

Young nodded weakly. "Be happy!" he said to Eiko. Then he bowed to us and left.

A few days after Eiko's wedding, we learned Young had hanged himself. In his suicide note he wrote:

I've lost face so much, I can't live any longer.

And so ended the life of a kind and decent man.

By the time my father went to see his body, it had already been taken away by the secret police.

His wife committed suicide a few days later.

I don't know how many returnees experienced such tragedies. I expect there were countless stories like these. Some were sent to concentration camps. Others were purged or executed. So many lives wasted.

When my sister Hifumi was of "marriageable age," as they used to say, another kind man, Lee Song-rak, helped find her a husband. Lee had worked in the publicity department of the League of Koreans in Japan and had brought transmission equipment with him from Japan when he moved to North Korea. He contributed a great deal to the party and was publicly recognized and admired for his efforts. He was also a warmhearted person. When he learned that Hifumi was eligible for marriage, he contacted a returnee who lived in Wonsan. Not long after that, my sister married him. I didn't like Hifumi's new husband at all. I thought he was lazy, and I resented his coming over to our house all the time to ask for food for his parents when we had hardly enough food to survive ourselves. My mother worried that if she refused, he would be cruel to Hifumi, so she asked the villagers to give us food to help out. I couldn't stand the fact that she was begging on his account. Eventually we couldn't keep it up any longer, and they ended up moving to Pujon.

Meanwhile, Lee was assigned to a transmission-equipment factory in Sinanju. Then, one day, he was suddenly denounced as a traitor because he'd married a woman from South Korea. The real issue had nothing to do with his wife, of course—they'd known about her all along; it was just that he'd attempted to make improvements in his new post. Lee became persona non grata and was dismissed from his post. Just like that, he became a nonperson. I later heard that his family split up, and he became a vagrant who could be seen loitering around the Sinanju train station.

My father's friends were disappearing one by one. Kim Uu-yon was another one who came to a sad end. He was a returnee who used to run a laundry in Kawasaki back in Japan. Like my father, he was married to a Japanese woman. In North Korea, Kim became a bus driver. One day, during a break, he started talking to his colleagues about his life in Japan. A few days later, he and his wife were picked up by the secret police and whisked off to Yodok concentration camp, a notorious hellhole. After ten years—an eternity in a place like that—his wife was released and came to live near our house. She'd been a cheerful person before, but now she was completely numb and empty. Her face was expressionless, her voice devoid of any feeling. She avoided contact with people at all costs. She'd become yet another nonperson living among us.

One day, she turned up at our house, carrying her son. We were stunned, since she made such a point of avoiding people. It turned out that her son was desperately ill. I carried him on my back to the village clinic.

"His tongue is festering, and he hasn't been able to eat for three days. Could you give him a penicillin G injection?" I asked the doctor.

I didn't know whether penicillin would work, but in North Korea, that was the only antibiotic there was. I thought it was probably his only chance at survival.

"What? You want me to treat him for free? Impudent prick! Why should I use up valuable medicine on him? Pay up, or at least bring me some medicinal herbs! Then we'll talk."

Health care in North Korea is supposedly free, but in reality it isn't free at all. Poor people can't get treatment without some form of payment. If you don't have any money—bring some alcohol. Bring some cigarettes. Bring some Chinese medicine. Or forget it.

I noticed a framed quotation on the clinic wall behind the doctor. It said, "Medicine is a benevolent art. A doctor must be a greater Communist than anybody." The words of Kim Il-sung.

Suddenly, I was burning with rage. And something cracked inside me.

"Who do you actually treat? No one at all?" I yelled.

And with that, I punched him. It was as if a dam had burst inside me. All the years of misery and hopelessness came rushing out. Suddenly I was on top of him, whaling on him with my fists. But even that wasn't enough. My anger was boiling over. I ran back to my house to grab a knife. I really wanted to kill the guy. A doctor who didn't help people was worse than useless—he was a mockery of everything he stood for. When I got back to the clinic, several police officers were standing in the corridor. I considered killing them too. But suddenly, out of nowhere, my father appeared and wrested the knife from my hand.

He told me to get out of there. Suddenly the reality of what I had been about to do came crashing down on me. I ran home.

My father stayed at the clinic for a while, and then he came home. Three days later, he had to report to the police station, but again he came back unscathed. I have no idea what happened. He never told me. But it must have been something good, because I wasn't arrested and nothing ever came of it.

I used to hate violence, especially since I had witnessed my father brutally beating my mother when I was a child. But after the confrontation with the doctor, my attitude changed. Violence began to seem like the only answer. I felt so helpless as I stood by, watching good people being purged and exiled and destroyed. My mother advised me to cool my temper. Otherwise, I'd disappear too.

In the seventies, a new slogan appeared: "Speed strategy!" This became yet another meaningless mouthful repeated ad nauseam at our study meetings. We also had to memorize Kim Il-sung's Ten Commandments and then repeat them endlessly until they were chiseled into our brains for all time. In the end, I felt as though my very mind had been occupied.

I can remember those commandments to this day. Well, of course I can. I'd have been dead long ago if I couldn't. Here they are:

1. Thou shalt give thy all in the struggle to unify the entire society with the revolutionary ideology of the Great Leader Comrade Kim Il-sung.
2. Thou shalt honor the Great Leader Comrade Kim Il-sung with all thy loyalty.
3. Thou shalt make absolute the authority of the Great Leader Comrade Kim Il-sung.
4. Thou shalt make the Great Leader Comrade Kim Il-sung's revolutionary ideology thy faith and make his instructions thy creed.

5. Thou shalt adhere strictly to the principle of unconditional obedience in carrying out the Great Leader Comrade Kim Il-sung's instructions.

6. Thou shalt strengthen the entire party's ideology and willpower and revolutionary unity, centering on the Great Leader Comrade Kim Il-sung.

7. Thou shalt learn from the Great Leader Comrade Kim Il-sung and adopt the Communist look, revolutionary work methods, and people-oriented work style.

8. Thou shalt value the political life thou wast given by the Great Leader Comrade Kim Il-sung, and loyally repay his great trust and thoughtfulness with heightened political awareness and skill.

9. Thou shalt establish strong organizational regulations so that the entire party, nation, and military move as one under the one and only leadership of the Great Leader Comrade Kim Il-sung.

10. Thou shalt pass down the great achievement of the revolution by the Great Leader Comrade Kim Il-sung from generation to generation, inheriting and completing it even unto the very end.

Much later, I checked out the Ten Commandments of the Abrahamic religions. You know how many of them contain a reference to God? About five. So it seems that God could learn a thing or two from the Great Leader Comrade Kim Il-sung, peace be upon him.

In practical terms, the new "speed strategy" meant that we had to create farms wherever there was soil and turn mountains into terraced fields. To achieve this, more laborers were needed.

In the spring of 1970, I was sent to work at a cooperative farm near Chongpyong-ri. I drove a tractor with a trailer carrying three other laborers, jolting our way slowly to our destination.

When we got to the farm, we boarded a military truck. After thirty minutes or so, we came to a deep valley where soldiers and farm laborers were already hard at work on the side of the mountain. We reported our arrival and were issued work pants. This was the very first new pair of pants I had received since coming to North Korea. I took off my ratty pants and put on the new pair. I was elated. You'd have thought I'd won the lottery.

At five o'clock the next morning, a bugle sounded to wake us from our long hut, which was designed like a military barracks. After roll call, we formed a line and ran down to the river at the heart of the valley. We broke through the frozen river with rocks, dipped our hands in, and washed our faces. The icy water stung my face and instantly numbed my hands. After that, we ran to the army post. Wonder of wonders, we were given white rice in the mess hut. I hadn't tasted white rice for ages. In fact, the sight of that white rice nearly brought several of us to tears. I didn't want to leave the mess hall, ever. But we had to get to work.

Our job was to remove the rocks and piles of earth that the military had dug out of the mountainside as they worked to build tunnels throughout the area. The tunnels were being built to house gunpowder and munitions factories. During the Korean War, these plants had been destroyed by American aerial bombardments, so it made sense to build their replacements underground. However, the power lines, also underground, didn't work properly. The voltage was too low, so some factories couldn't operate. It goes without saying that clearing away the rubble left by the tunnel construction was backbreaking work.

After a few weeks, I got a telegram from Kan Ki-son, Eiko's husband. WEDDING JAN. 25. COME HOME BY 24TH, it said. I had no idea whose wedding it was. Then I thought that maybe something terrible had happened at home, something that couldn't be addressed explicitly, and the wedding reference was a code. So many tragedies had befallen our family that I always assumed the worst.

So I returned to my workplace in the mountains of sand and rubble and told the guy in charge about the telegram. Over the sound of dynamite exploding and bits drilling into bedrock, he shouted, "You can go." So I dashed off, hopped in the tractor, and drove back to Dong Chong-ri as quickly as the vehicle would go. I mulled over all my worst fears as I drove. I didn't feel relieved to be leaving, despite the difficulty of the work and the harsh conditions. At least there was guaranteed food. Along with my new pair of pants, I'd been given a new pair of military boots—the first footgear that actually fit me since I'd arrived in North Korea.

When I got home, the wedding preparations were in the works. There were some rice cakes, meat and fish, sake, and a few other offerings. I didn't know what was going on, so I just stood there, taking it all in. Then, Kan's mother came up to me. "Great news! It's your wedding day," she said.

You could have knocked me over with a feather. To say I was surprised doesn't begin to describe how I felt. I was dumbfounded. Paralyzed with shock.

The woman I was apparently about to marry was called Lee He-suku. Her father was the vice manager of a power plant in Hamhung City. Her eyesight was terrible, and . . . well, I'm sorry to say this, but she wasn't exactly beautiful.

"Do you think that just because I'm a returnee and very poor, I can't find my own wife? Is that why you've found one for me?"

My father was sitting next to Kan's mother. I soon learned that *he* was the one who'd asked her to find me a wife. But even he seemed to think this setup was too cruel.

The truth gradually came out. It was He-suku's stepmother who was in such a hurry for the wedding to take place. This marriage was a great chance for the woman to get rid of her stepdaughter. I later learned that the woman had never liked He-suku and often bullied and tormented her. Kan's mother didn't know anything about that, so I can't really blame her. I just didn't know what to do. In the end, it quite frankly felt like too much trouble to put a stop to it. I simply didn't have the energy to put up a fight, and my options were quite limited. So I went through with it. I was twenty-three years old.

A few days after the wedding, I was preparing breakfast when my father came up to me.

"I realize now that it was very wrong of me to ask Kan's mother to find a woman for you. You're my only son, and I want you to be happy. You'd better get divorced and find the right woman."

"She hasn't got anywhere to go. It's done now. Let her stay with me. I'll look after her," I said.

"As you wish. Take care of her, then. But I can't accept her as my daughter-in-law. And if you're going to live with her, you'll have to find somewhere else to live."

How's that for irony?

I can't say I loved He-suku. I hardly knew her. I soon discovered that her stepmother had kept her locked up in a room at home, so she'd never really learned to do anything. She couldn't cook, and she spent many hours daydreaming. But I couldn't imagine living on my own, especially in such a hard world, and she desperately needed my help. So we decided to make a go of it and move in together.

My mother came up to me when I was packing my belongings.

"Your destiny is always so hard," she said, a sad expression on her face. I didn't know what to say. I hated to leave her, but I had to fulfill my obligations to my new wife.

I found an old couple in Dong Chong-ri who had a spare room they said we could use. Of course, there were conditions. We had to give them part of our food rations, help collect firewood, do some household chores, and the like. It wasn't long before the old couple started increasing their demands. Worst of all, what they wanted most of all was anything of value from Japan. They couldn't understand why, as a returnee, I didn't have anything. But of course, we had nothing to give them.

That first year was a big adjustment. In addition to my regular farm job, I now had to look after our landlords. In addition, my wife became pregnant. I worried constantly about how I was going to provide for a child when we were barely surviving ourselves. But I had no answers to that question. I just kept going to work, day after day, hoping for some kind of miracle.

About a year after we'd gotten married, I came home from work one day and suddenly felt dizzy. I lay down on the floor and started bleeding from my nose and ears. The bleeding wouldn't stop, and my wife panicked. I started losing consciousness, so I asked her to call for help.

I woke up in the hospital two days later. When I opened my eyes, I discovered my parents' worried faces gazing down at me. My nose and ears were stuffed with gauze. I looked around for He-suku, but she wasn't there.

"Your wife was so shocked when she saw you lose consciousness that she apparently—she—er—ran away," my father said.

I started to cry.

"Be strong," my mother said.

I didn't have time to consider the matter further, as just then I was distracted by a flash of pain. The bleeding turned out to be the result of a damaged blood vessel between my eyes. The doctor had given me an injection to stop the bleeding, but it didn't work. In the end, they inserted a roll of cotton gauze into my nose up to my eyes, and the bleeding stopped.

Once I left the hospital, my wife came to see me at my parents' house. Her stomach was very big, and it looked as though she was having difficulty walking.

"Please divorce me. I don't want to give you any more trouble. But our baby . . ." She didn't finish the sentence. I was wondering how she planned to raise a baby by herself.

My father leaped in. "Don't worry!" he said. "We'll bring up the baby."

It would be his first grandchild.

My first son was born on March 25, 1972. We named him Ho-chol. He-suku gave birth to him in our home. She left shortly after he was born. I want to say that I was sad to see her go, but we had hardly known each other. Perhaps it was for the best. Besides, I had more pressing concerns. I had a son to look after. Of course, there were no soft towels and no powdered milk—not much of anything, really. Even as I focused on meeting my son's immediate daily needs, I couldn't help but think about this tiny, innocent baby's future. He wouldn't be given much. His life would be full of struggle and heartbreak. I should have been thrilled to be a father, but I couldn't see much to be happy about. I felt pained that his life would be so full of suffering. My parents and youngest sister were pleased, however, and I was happy to move back in with them.

Two months had passed since the birth of my son, and my mother was preparing breakfast in the kitchen. She had once been quite tall, but she'd shrunk over the years. Her work pants had holes in them where her skin showed through. She was only forty-seven years old, but she looked ancient.

Suddenly she seemed to lose her balance. She turned and staggered toward me as I held my son.

"I need to take a little rest," she said to me as she sat down beside me. She looked at my son and me with a little smile on her lips. I noticed she was struggling to breathe, and I started to panic.

"When you go back to Japan, please take my ashes with you," she said in a thin, raspy voice. "Take them to your grandparents. Put them in their family grave."

"What are you talking about? Stop talking like that. It's a bad omen. You have a new grandson."

But her face only grew more flushed. I knew then that something was very wrong. Her breathing grew shallow and labored, and her face grew paler by the second.

"I'm going to take a little nap," she said, lying down.

I started to rub her back since I knew that she liked that. "Are you in pain? Do you feel sick?" I asked, unsure what to do.

But she didn't respond. I shook her, but she didn't react at all.

"Mother!" I shouted. "Mother!"

But there was no answer.

And then the baby started wailing.

My father and sister rushed into the room, disturbed from their sleep.

A trail of tears trickled from the corners of my mother's eyes.

My father put his hand to her mouth.

Then he looked at me with a blank expression.

I could hear what he was saying, but his words made no sense to me.

"She's dead."

The only person who came to our house when word of my mother's death spread through the village was Mrs. Chon, the wife of the man who'd helped us build our house so many years ago after the fire. She rushed in and shook my mother's body, tears streaming down her face.

"You just became a grandmother! Why did you have to die?" she wailed.

My son, worn out with crying, was sleeping in my arms.

That night, Eiko and Hifumi came over. Eiko took the baby from me. She could see that I was numb and distracted.

"You're the first son. You have to be strong," she said to me.

Hifumi said the same thing.

As I looked at my mother's frail body, I was struck by her ratty, hole-ridden pants. I felt so sorry for her. I mean, she had died in those decrepit, tattered work pants. I couldn't bear it.

I walked out into the dark night. It was a cloudy evening, so the stars and moon were completely obscured. I wandered around the village for about an hour, and then I went past a house where I saw a pair of pants hanging out to dry. Whispering to myself that I would never do such a thing again and begging forgiveness for my actions, I grabbed those pants and shoved them under my shirt.

I ran home, washed my mother's body, and put them on her. And guess what. Those pants turned out to be ratty too.

We placed her in her coffin the following afternoon. I tried to hammer the lid down, but the stupid nails were inferior and wouldn't go in straight. To me, that said it all. As for my mother, she hadn't enjoyed a single luxury since she'd moved to North Korea. I couldn't stop thinking about it. Had she experienced a single good day in her entire life? Or had her whole life been no better than her ragged work pants? Tattered pants . . . wretched life. Even as I carried her coffin, I mulled over whether she'd been granted a single day of pure happiness. But I couldn't think of one. Maybe she could finally be happy in death.

We buried her on a mountainside near a fruit farm and put up a simple piece of wood to mark the spot. "Here lies Miyoko Ishikawa," it said. My father couldn't speak. He just sighed with grief.

When we got back to our house, the villagers who had helped carry her coffin as far as the mountainside were there, partaking enthusiastically of the food and drink that Eiko had provided. It made me sick. When my mother was alive, they never gave her the time of day. Now, here they were, eating and drinking in honor of her death. I couldn't bear the hypocrisy of their actions—why didn't they just go and dance on her grave?

I went back to my mother's resting place. I lit a cigarette and placed it on her grave instead of incense. And I sang a children's song that my mother used to sing to me called "Red Dragonfly." She would sing it while looking up at the sky, saying that only the sky connected her to her mother country. She always cried when she sang it. I could barely get out the words through my sobs. Overwhelmed by grief and despair, I wanted to sink into the ground with her.

Life went on. It wasn't the same, but my father, my youngest sister, Masako, my son, and I remained together. Masako became a farm laborer. My father, nearing sixty at the time, was still in charge of the boiler in a fruit-processing factory. Meanwhile, I continued my work on the farm.

We usually got up at five o'clock. For breakfast, we ate Chinese cabbage that we grew in our garden. It was boiled in water and thickened with cornstarch. Sounds pretty ghastly, right? It was. But if we could get down a bowlful of the stuff, it made our stomachs feel full.

My father used to leave the house first. Then I'd carry my son off to try to find someone who could breast-feed him. I'd go from house to house, asking for help. I couldn't pay anything, so all I could do was hope to find some kindhearted soul. People sometimes shouted at me. I burned with shame, but what else could I do? Let him starve? So I never gave up. After that, I'd take him to the day nursery at the farm and start work.

Ever since the house fire, we'd never had so much as a single futon between us. We just slept on the floor. It was difficult to get to sleep in the cold house, especially for my infant son. My father and I would take off our shirts and snuggle close to him to keep him warm with our body heat. We'd take him to the warmest place near the heating stove.

And when the stove gave out, we'd cuddle him again and take him to the cooking stove and lie down there.

He often cried from hunger during the night. I'd make a thin rice gruel of cornstarch and rice powder and give him a few spoonfuls in an attempt to assuage his constant hunger. But sometimes that didn't work, so I'd carry him around on my back to try to pacify him. Sometimes I fell asleep standing up. And then, if my knees gave, the jolt would wake him and make him cry even more. In the end, I leaned against the wall and slept like that. He could so easily have died—from hunger, from exhaustion, from the cold. I lived in a constant state of fear and dread and helplessness as there was so little I could do for him.

Life was just as hard, even harder than before, but my son took my mind off my mother's death. Apart from him, I had nothing to live for. And if I thought too much about that, well, I moved toward the abyss. So I struggled desperately just to make it from one day to the next.

CHAPTER 4

During that time, the world seemed completely unforgiving. I was a single father at age twenty-six, divorced after a meaningless marriage that had lasted a year. My mother had died young after a lifetime of misery. My father and I struggled to keep my son from the jaws of death. And all around me, I saw nothing but a kind of farcical futility. I could no longer really see the point of being alive.

So what did I do when I reached this new low? Human beings are nothing if not irrational, so I did what countless people had done before me and countless others will do long after I'm dead: I prayed. It didn't even matter that I didn't really believe in God. I prayed that no more tragedies would befall me. I prayed for my son's health. I prayed for a change of fortune. I prayed every single day. And God watched over me. For five years. For five years, nothing happened to me at all. And then I turned thirty-one.

And God got bored again.

It was autumn, just after the harvest. Food-distribution day was coming up, the one time of year you could relax a little. I came home from work one day and found my sister Masako cuddling my son. She was crying inconsolably. I took him in my arms and asked her what was wrong with him, but he was fine. He too was wondering why Masako was upset. "Why are you crying, Auntie?" he asked. No answer. She just continued to sob. Then she suddenly stopped crying and looked at me very seriously. "Masaji, please don't get angry with me," she said. "I'm pregnant." I was stunned, having had no inkling she was even seeing anyone.

"Who is he? Are you planning to get married?" I asked.

And then it all came tumbling out. His name was Han Om-choru, and he was a farm laborer from the village. He had been all doting and sweet when my sister was willing to do what he asked, but as soon as she told him she was pregnant, he changed his tune. When she had asked him if he intended to marry her, his family had gotten involved. Then it was the usual story. Of course he couldn't marry her—she was a Japanese bastard. And with that, they'd pushed her out of the house.

I could feel the rage building inside me as she told me the story. My mother had always admonished me to watch my temper and be patient; to her mind, violence was never the solution. But I just couldn't bear it. Masako was my sister, and they were disrespecting her.

Holding an ax in my hand, I went to Han's house, about a ten-minute walk from ours. I found him outside.

"You've taken advantage of my sister, you brute! Well, you know what, asshole? You can't get away with that."

His family tried to restrain me, but I grabbed him by the back of the neck and pulled him down to the ground. He looked scared to death and burst into tears. Then he cried, "Forgive me! I'll take full responsibility!" But I was beyond reason and just beat the living daylights out of him. I knew better, but I couldn't control myself.

Even as I pummeled him with my fists, I still couldn't get rid of my anger. I guess my mother was right; you can't solve anything with violence. But I had been told my whole life that since I was Japanese, I was less than human. I'd had enough. Eventually Han's family managed to pull me off him. I was weary of fighting by that point and stumbled off toward home.

Incredibly, Hifumi's husband found someone willing to marry Masako. He was an accountant working in a school in a town called Mensan, deep in the mountains. His wife had died, and he had two kids. A returnee, of course. I sensed trouble from the outset since she'd never even laid eyes on him. Having gone through that myself, I was skeptical about whether it was really the right solution for her. But Masako was happy to go ahead with it. I guess she was willing to do anything for a chance at a stable life.

On the day she left, I said to her, "If he treats you badly, just let me know. I'll take care of it."

"No thanks," she said. "No more violence. Promise you'll try to stay coolheaded."

My father and I felt lonely without her around, as did my son. It felt strange not to have a woman in the house. My father started asking me if I was interested in getting married again. I wasn't exactly enthusiastic, but when I thought of my son and my future, I knew deep down that I wanted to find someone to share my life with. Maybe it would work out the second time round.

In 1976, I met a woman by the name of Kim Te-sul. We'd both come to North Korea from Japan in the sixties, and we were both divorced. She'd previously been married to a native North Korean, but her mother-in-law bullied her constantly: "You're a returnee. Why haven't you got anything of value?" So her marriage had lasted all of two months. Because we'd been through similar painful experiences, we thought we could share our feelings and spend a peaceful life together.

The wedding ceremony was very simple. We shared what little food we had, and Te-sul and I had a cup of sake to mark our pledge to each other. After the ceremony, my father told me that Te-sul would have to leave for a while to look after her bedridden grandmother in Hamju. So we wouldn't even begin our married life under the same roof.

Te-sul, her sister, and her brother had been brought to North Korea by their grandmother after their father was killed in an accident in Japan. After his death, their mother had disappeared, so their grandmother was left to raise them. Her grandmother had no one else to help her at the time, so we agreed to live separately for a while. I understood the difficulty of Te-sul's situation, and so we saw each other when we could, taking the forty-five-minute train ride to visit as often as possible.

The new year came. Spring came. It was 1975. One day, I saw a woman standing outside the house when I came home from work. She was wearing tattered work pants and had two kids in tow. She looked so disheveled, I thought from a distance she might be a homeless person. When I got closer, I noticed she was pregnant. And then she turned to me. It was Masako.

"What are *you* doing here? You look terrible. What's happened?" I asked.

She just looked at me and burst into tears. I took her inside, and through her sobs, she explained to me how her mother-in-law had bullied her. Once again, it was the same old story.

"You're a returnee. Why haven't you got anything?" her mother-in-law had said. "Our relations in Japan send us money and things. Why don't yours?"

Her new husband soon joined in. Eventually, they forced her and his two kids—*his* two kids, mind you, from his first wife who had died—out of the house.

She had no money and no options. She started stealing food. And then she started walking—pregnant, with two kids, age nine and seven, in tow—all the way back to our village. It took them three weeks. No wonder she was such a wreck. I felt full of despair and sadness for her—but also helpless to make her life better. I prayed to God and begged him to help her.

One month later, Masako gave birth to a boy, whom she named Gang-ho. She was too weak and thin to breast-feed him, so we gave him some rice water, but it didn't do any good. Soon, his feces turned black, so I took him to the clinic. The doctor was a nice man, nothing like the doctor I'd punched before, but there was nothing he could do. "I'm really sorry," he said, "but you'll just have to wait and see if he gets better on his own."

Autumn descended, and the weather began to turn cool. The baby's cries had grown very feeble by then. And then one night, he died. He was just shy of three months old. My sister wept and wept. She cried until she was utterly exhausted. Then she fell asleep, and when she awoke, she started wailing again.

I wrapped the baby's body in a cloth and carried him out into the night. Loud thunder and heavy rain soon followed, appropriately enough. I walked past my mother's grave, past the fruit farm, and climbed the mountain, his pitiful corpse in my arms. Rainwater gushed down the side of the mountain, washing away the earth and sand.

I kept stumbling and slipping on the muddy ground. Finally I stopped and placed the tiny body on the ground. I started digging with my bare hands. I tried not to think about anything as I dug and dug in the darkness. Whenever the lightning flashed, I could see the baby's body beside me. A ghastly, tragic sight. It was the last straw.

I stood up and shouted into the void, "Why do we have to bear such suffering? What did we do to deserve this?" Hot tears coursed down my already soaked face.

I buried the baby and headed back down the mountain, bellowing like the lunatic I'd become.

After my nephew died, I kept asking myself the same question again and again: Why did my mother and an innocent baby have to die? What point was there to a life that consisted entirely of pain? Ever since coming to North Korea, I had experienced only cruelty, starvation, and despair. I was done with people.

So I decided to stop working on the cooperative farm and become a charcoal burner deep in the mountains. As a charcoal burner, I would be able to work completely on my own and live like a hermit. Of course, I thought of my son, my father, and my sisters. But I was in such a bad state of mind that I feared it might be worse for everyone if I stuck around.

I didn't have the right to choose a new job just like that, of course. I needed to get permission. If you wanted to be transferred to another job, you had to be issued a party job-transfer permit, a ration-transfer permit, and a military job-transfer permit. Your food ration came from your workplace, so if you stopped working, you simply starved. Then again, as in any totalitarian state, some people just dropped out of society completely. But if you did that, you had only two choices. You could become a homeless vagrant, or you could become a bandit.

There was, however, a loophole in all this bureaucracy. If it was decided that you were not worth monitoring, you could end up completely ignored. The party figured you weren't worth the trouble. That's how I ended up when I left my sanctioned job. The party didn't seem to care whether I was alive or dead. To them, I ceased to exist altogether.

By most people's standards, being a charcoal burner was one of the worst jobs. It was as tough as being a farm laborer or coal miner, a job for the lowest of the low. If you chose to stop working as a tractor driver to be a charcoal burner instead, people thought you were crazy. But that worked in my favor, you see. As soon as I handed in my application to be a charcoal burner, it was accepted immediately. A first! "A *charcoal burner? Nobody* wants to do that!"

My father and sister were both resigned to my decision. They seemed to realize that I wouldn't change my mind no matter what they said. They could sense I was barely keeping it together. So when I asked them to take care of my son, they didn't protest. He was six years old at the time. Every day he used to come home from school and tell me all about the things he'd learned, who said what and who did what and so on, wide-eyed with his child's sense of wonder. His sweetness was utterly heartbreaking. I also felt sorry to be leaving my wife, who was still looking after her grandmother, but it heartened me that I wouldn't need to communicate with anyone from now on. It would be better for them, and for me—at least that's how I thought about it at the time.

On the morning of my departure, my father and sister stood together awkwardly to see me off, looking forlorn. Just as I was about to leave, my son said innocently, "I'll take care of Grandfather and Aunt. Please make lots of money."

As I hugged him close to me, I felt my heart breaking. I started to walk away from them, and I didn't look back. I knew that if I did, I would fall apart.

I walked from early morning until dusk, getting lost several times along the way. Eventually, I arrived at the work station.

The work station consisted of three kilns and tents for the workers to live in and an ox for transport. There were only seven or eight workers, which suited me just fine. All of their faces were deeply lined, their wrinkles and scars telling the stories of all the trouble in their lives.

I started work the next day. As instructed, I cut down a beech tree, chopped off the branches, and cut it into twenty-inch lengths. Then I took them to the kiln. I packed the kiln with the cut-up branches and lit a fire in the center. After making sure the fire took, I covered the kiln entrance with soil. Soon after that, smoke began rising out of the chimney. I was told if the smoke was yellow, then the fire was strong enough and that the fire had to burn for three days inside the kiln. When the smoke stopped coming out of the chimney, you had to wait another three days before retrieving the charcoal, so the whole process generally took about a week.

The work was supposed to be done by two people, but in reality it was usually done single-handedly. That suited me just fine. When my first batch of charcoal was ready, I broke the soil around the entrance and crawled into the kiln. It was the first time I'd ever done it, so I wanted to check whether it was successful without anyone else around. I wore a wet towel over my mouth, but it fell off inside the kiln, so a lot of charcoal powder got into my nose and mouth. And it was so hot, I began sweating profusely. I was shocked at how quickly my energy drained away, but I loaded my basket with charcoal and crawled back out.

Kim, the leader of the group, looked concerned when I emerged. "Be careful! There's poisonous gas in there," he warned.

I didn't know it at the time, but it was unusual for someone to speak out like that. Everyone at the work station had troubled backgrounds, and no one was inclined to make conversation, even about mundane things. Silence was the rule.

My meals consisted of corn rice, which I brought from my encampment every day, together with some mountain weeds, which I picked and boiled. Apparently, alcohol was essential to this job. God knows if this is true or not, because I've found absolutely no medical evidence to support this theory whatsoever, but I was told that if I didn't drink alcohol, I'd suffer from lung disease. I'd never really drunk much alcohol before, but I sure got to know its taste quickly. If alcohol wasn't included in our rations, all hell broke loose. "No alcohol, no work!" some of the laborers chanted. So the supply remained remarkably steady.

When I'd been doing the job for about three months, the forest warden made an appearance one day. Some trees had been cut down without permission, and he was a bit scared, so he asked me to join him on his patrol that night. Just after sunset we set out, and, sure enough, we came upon some people chopping down a tree.

"Don't move! Stay right where you are!" the warden yelled as he ran toward them with his feeble flashlight. There were about eight young guys gathered around the tree. I expected them to run off, but they didn't. Quite the opposite, in fact. They turned on the warden and started beating him up. I jumped in to help, and eventually all eight of them were laid out.

After that, I was the talk of the nearby village. They called me "the wrestler." Not exactly "Tiger" like my father, but I didn't mind.

A few days later, a policeman turned up, asking for my fingerprints. I couldn't believe it. I admit that I may have gone a bit too far, but I was helping the warden, not attacking him. I bit my tongue, not wanting to get myself in deeper trouble. I could guess what had happened. The warden had been bribed by the thieves to allow them to chop a few trees here and there, and the warden had led me into a trap. I'd become a charcoal burner to avoid the liars and thieves who passed themselves off as good people in North Korea. But there was no escape.

Just as I was getting used to my job, I got a telegram from my wife. It was short and to the point. Son born April 15. Come back soon.

My emotions were tangled, and my mind was cloudy. Masako's baby had died. I'd gone slightly mad and taken off to live as a hermit. And my new life suited me just fine. But now a new baby was in the picture. Part of me was thrilled by the news. But another part of me . . . less so.

When I told my boss the news, he was so ecstatic, you'd have thought the baby was his. He produced a big bag of glutinous rice, sesame seeds, azuki beans, and a load of regular rice, all scrounged from the emergency food supply.

"You must go. Best wishes to your wife from me!" he said.

I was stunned. I don't think I'd ever seen him so much as smile before. He never spoke much and was generally aloof. But that day, he couldn't have been kinder. I set off walking for home, surprised and confused but happy at the thought of bringing these precious gifts to my wife.

I arrived at my wife's place on the nineteenth, and my brother-in-law welcomed me into the house. My wife was dozing with my newborn son asleep next to her. When she awoke, she was so happy to see me that she cried.

"I didn't think you'd come," she said.

I'd been away for more than six months, and she thought I'd left her for good.

The baby was born on Kim Il-sung's birthday. That was hardly a happy omen to me. Not only did he have the misfortune of being born on that wretched man's birthday, but it was also the date on which our first house had burned down in 1964. On the other hand, it was also the date that the annual food rations were distributed, so maybe it was not all bad.

My wife told me the story of the baby's birth. She and her brother had received some glutinous rice in honor of our Leader's birthday. They'd steamed it and were pounding it to make rice cakes—a rare treat—when suddenly, my wife went into labor.

She broke off the story and paused awkwardly for a moment. "I'm sorry," she said. "I named the baby Myong-hwa. I would have waited to discuss it with you, but I didn't think you were coming back."

Surprised, I said, "But in the telegram . . . you told me it was a boy."

My wife looked at me apologetically. "I know. It's just I thought . . . well, if I told you it was a girl . . . you wouldn't come back to see her."

"Don't be silly! Boy . . . girl . . . they're both lovely."

I was so happy, I pounded some steamed glutinous rice, added some sweet azuki beans, and made a special dessert. We invited some neighbors over to celebrate the birth.

Seeing my baby's face as she slept so peacefully made me determined to work harder than ever. But the reality hit home late that night. I had a wife. And now two children. And however hard I worked, I would always be poor. I would never be allowed to better myself, no matter how much effort I put in. My children would be faced with a life of hardship regardless of what I did.

I woke up the next day, all my naive excitement drained away. Once again, I found myself overwhelmed by a sense of futility. My wife noticed the change in me. I could see it in her face. But she didn't say anything.

I decided to visit my father and sister and my son.

Ho-chol was thrilled to see me. He kept following me around; he didn't want me to be out of his sight for a minute. Kids are like that—they can break your heart with a smile. My father had already met baby Myong-hwa, and he was over the moon about her. Masako was there, still looking bereft. She was working in the fruit-juice plant in Dong Chong-ri, but it hadn't seemed to improve her state of mind much. At first, it was great to be back, but the sense of hopelessness returned soon enough. I couldn't help but think that if another tragedy befell my family, I wouldn't be able to carry on.

I decided to get out of the house and take a walk around the village. As chance would have it, I bumped into a few old acquaintances. They'd always despised me, but strangely, they felt the need to chat. They told me about a new woman who'd turned up in the village. Apparently, she was a rich returnee from Japan, recently banished from Hamhung. Her lifestyle in Hamhung had been so luxurious, she'd fallen afoul of the secret police and been banished to our village, of all places. Normally she'd have been carted off to a concentration camp, but people thought she must have bribed someone.

I listened without much interest and wandered off. A few minutes later, I reached the village stream—and there she was, this mysterious lady. She was clean and elegant and well-dressed. I walked up to her and introduced myself. After all, we were both returnees. She glanced at me briefly, then studiously ignored me. It was clear that, to her, I simply didn't exist. She sailed past me obliviously, another ghost in that land of the dead.

It was then that I decided to go back to the kiln, back to a world of hard work and silence. Back to cutting down trees and branches and carrying them on my back, shoving them in the kiln, and drinking away the pain in my back and my heart. I just wanted to do something honest and pure, something I couldn't be reprimanded for. But somehow, even when I got back to my hermit's life, I couldn't help but think about that returnee who'd ignored me. It was stupid to dwell on that. Of all the insults I'd endured in my life, hers was hardly the worst. But I couldn't. She'd made a point of ignoring me. She'd acted as if I didn't exist at all, even when I stood right in front of her. That moment seemed to sum up my entire existence. I was nothing. Less than nothing. Whatever I did was a waste of time. A waste of effort.

As I was cutting down a tree one morning, I suddenly thought, *The hell with this! Just end it!* The pain of death would be nothing compared to this hell on earth.

I got hold of a rope—no shortage of ropes in the charcoal-burning business—slung it over a tree branch, and tied a noose. There was a rock beneath the branch just the right height for jumping off. I'd made sure of that. I climbed onto it and looked out at the river flowing in front of me. Rushing indifferently toward the future. For some reason, tears gushed from my eyes.

I pulled the noose over my head. Took a deep breath. Jumped.

The branch swayed violently above me. My body swung about. I writhed uncontrollably. But it was as if I'd stepped out of my body and was looking down on my contortions from above. I could still feel, still see, still breathe, although barely.

The fact was, I'd messed up my own suicide. I couldn't even get that right. The noose had gotten stuck around my chin, not all the way around my neck, so it couldn't constrict my carotid artery. I could breathe slightly, but doing so was painful and laborious. And my body, or something in my brain—I don't know—something struggled desperately to survive. Tears of pain and frustration streamed down my cheeks, and saliva drooled from my mouth.

And then I heard a shout behind me. It was Shin, one of my fellow charcoal burners.

I heard him run up, and suddenly he shoved his head up against my crotch. He hauled me onto his shoulders and pulled the noose from around my head. Then he collapsed, and we both fell to the ground.

I was still choking and writhing. I felt a wave of frustration and anguish that I hadn't been able to kill myself. I clawed at the ground and cursed myself. I was crying. Shin was crying. "Why would you do such a terrible thing?" he yelled through his tears.

Born again.

Shin must have told my boss what I'd done, because that night, my boss said to me, "What on earth were you thinking? If you die, what's going to happen to your family? If your children mean anything to you at all, you can't just abandon hope like that!"

I burst into tears and couldn't stop. I just kept sobbing.

"I guess I'm meant to keep crying," I said.

He laughed at me, but kindly.

We drank till late that night.

About a year passed. And then one day I got a telegram from my wife, telling me she could finally leave her grandmother's house. I decided it was time to go back. I asked my boss for permission, and he was very sympathetic. I felt as if I was returning from some kind of purgatory.

The day I left, all the guys saw me off. They were a taciturn bunch, but very kind. A swirl of mixed emotions ran through me. These men were the most honest people I'd met in a long time. We lived in a mutually agreeable silence together, in a realm that seemed somehow removed from the petty realities of daily life. But I had a family to attend to, and I felt some small seed of hope taking root deep inside. I was ready to go.

I returned to my father's place in Dong Chong-ri, and my wife and baby daughter came to live with us. There were eight of us in the house now: my sister Masako, her two stepchildren, my son, my wife, my daughter, my father, and I. Eight! And my father was the only person who was working, as my new job hadn't been assigned yet. It was practically impossible to get by.

It was the early eighties, and the food situation went from bad to worse. A common slogan at the time was "Communism means rice!" It was repeated all over. Farm laborers and students worked together to make terraced rice fields on mountainsides. But when the rainy season came, most of the fields were washed away due to poor planning. Even the fields that survived weren't in good enough shape to grow anything properly. Oh, and we still had to plant the seedlings very close to one another so that, in the end, the plants just crowded one another out and couldn't produce a decent crop. Despite knowing better, we all had to follow the ludicrous *Juche* system. If your farm didn't meet its target harvest, the farm manager fudged the account to make it look as if the target had actually been met. But despite all the fairy-tale record keeping, the supply didn't lie: the food ration distributed every autumn was growing smaller and smaller.

I asked an old lady who lived near the river with a mentally handicapped son if my family could stay in one of the rooms in her house. She agreed. So in the new year, my wife and I and our two children left my father's place. I still didn't have a job—I just couldn't find one no matter how hard I tried—so we survived on mountain weeds and fish from the river.

I desperately wanted to build a house for my family, so I borrowed some tools and an oxcart from the farm. It was snowing pretty heavily, but I couldn't stand it anymore. So I set off for the mountain. In the forest, the snow reached up to my waist in places, and it was a struggle even to walk through it. When I found a pine tree about eight inches in diameter, I chopped it down, put it in the oxcart, and hauled it back down the mountain. I did this again and again. It was exhausting work.

All I had to eat was some frozen corn rice I'd gotten from my father. Whenever I got thirsty, I shoved snow into my mouth. Every time I trudged up the mountain to chop down a tree, I sweated like mad. Then I shivered all the way back down. By the time I had enough trees, my tattered work pants were frozen with sweat and snow. When I walked, they rustled and sprinkled tiny ice crystals on the ground.

I peeled the bark off the trees with a sickle and piled all the logs near where I intended to build the house. I cut the trees into sections of the right length. Then I collected some stones by the river and dragged them back in the cart for the foundation. After laying the foundation stones, I put up the pillars. I used clay and mud to make a kind of plaster. If I'd been a party bigwig, I could've got hold of some cement, but that wasn't an option for me.

I mixed the plaster with my bare hands and slapped it on the logs. My palms were bleeding, so my blood was added to the mixture. I built a fire to warm my hands so that I could continue working. But the skin was peeling off my palms and the heat stung. It was all excruciating, but I just carried on. Day after day, week after week.

After five months, the house was just about done. I made an arch roof and covered it with some thatch my wife had made. It was more like a shack than a proper house, but at least it would offer us shelter from the rain. After studying the structure for a while, I turned to my wife.

"'Speed above all things' hasn't turned out so badly in this case!" I said.

"Speed above all things," she replied with a laugh. It was another of the times' ubiquitous slogans.

When we moved in, Ho-chol was seven years old; Myong-hwa was two. All we had was a box of apples and a rice pan my father had given us. Since I was no longer a farm laborer, I wasn't entitled to a food ration. So every day, I went off to the village farm and stole some daikon radishes. The dish we prepared from those was simple: Chop up the radish, including the leaves. Mix it all with a few grains of rice you've scrounged up. Add a lot of water to make rice gruel. Except it wasn't really rice gruel because there wasn't ever a single rice grain to be found when you ladled the ghastly stuff out. But even though we were indescribably poor, it was the first time I'd had my own family together, and somehow I thought we could survive. So "rice" gruel it was, every single day. I didn't feel bad about stealing the radishes. What choice did I have? My wife needed to eat in order to breast-feed our baby. My son had to eat, and so did I. It was simply a question of survival.

I developed a kind of "so what?" attitude. "Even if I could get a job, we still wouldn't be able to eat properly," I said to my wife. I decided we should live independently and not rely on the government. By the following spring, we were subsisting on dandelions, bracken, and mugwort. We boiled them with a paste made of acorns. Poisonous things, acorns, but there you go. The concoction tasted bitter, and our tongues went numb after eating it. But at least it had some kind of flavor, which seemed better than none at all.

In summer, I stole lots of thumb-size peaches, and we devoured them happily. Apples and potatoes too. I was not alone. Lots of other people were stealing stuff. I guess the police had given up.

Some of the food we ate had gone bad, and some of the weeds we consumed were poisonous. We often suffered from crippling stomachaches, but there was nothing we could do about it.

This kind of life went on for about a year until one day when my wife announced that she was worried about her grandmother. After that, she returned regularly to her house to see her and, often as not, she came back with a bag of rice. She told me her grandmother had given it to her, but I knew her grandmother wasn't wealthy. I also noticed that my wife looked weaker every time she returned home to us.

Eventually, I couldn't help but ask her how she was getting the rice.

At first, she didn't say anything, but I pressed her until she admitted the truth. Apparently, when she said she was going to her grandmother's house, she was really going to a blood-transfusion station in Hamhung City. She sold her blood to buy the rice.

I just gazed up at the sky.

Let me tell you what we were taught in school in North Korea. "People in South Korea can only survive by stealing things and selling their blood."

The irony!

It was June 1982, and my wife was in the final month of her second pregnancy. She'd had little to eat for months, just the usual weeds and wild plants. I'd seen her doubled up with stomach cramps countless times, but somehow she'd made it to this point. She was about to give birth.

We didn't have any money, so I couldn't take her to a clinic. I was desperate to find her some nutritious food—seaweed for soup and pork and rice to celebrate the birth—but those were far beyond our reach. Somehow I got hold of some eggs, a bag of rice, and some daikon radish leaves. I wanted to take great care of my wife, but that was the best I could do.

Kim went into labor in the morning on the fourth of June. I told her we should go to the hospital, but she insisted that she could give birth at home.

I noticed that her forehead was damp with sweat. I needed a soft cloth, but I had only one set of underwear and my wife had only two. All I could find was a worn-out rag.

As I boiled some water, she started groaning more loudly. I rubbed her back, but it didn't do much good. I got more worried as the hours passed.

"Shall I call a midwife?" I asked.

"I think the baby will come soon, so just stay with me," she said.

She kept repeating that and didn't want to listen to any of my suggestions. And I didn't want to leave her. I sent the kids off to walk to my father's place; Ho-chol had walked there many times, and I figured they would be safely out of the way there.

The room was scorching, with the boiling water, and I was sweating profusely. I could hardly imagine what it must have been like for my wife. She strained and writhed, but still the baby would not come. Before I knew it, the sun had set.

She clung to me and started to strain. Every time she strained, she lost a lot of blood. We were both covered with it. She was shuddering with constant pain, growing weaker by the moment. I poured some raw egg into her mouth to give her some energy, but it did little good. By ten o'clock that night, she was still bleeding and was practically unconscious.

"Come on, angel! You've gotta wake up! We need you. We need this baby. You can't give up on us now!" I cried.

She clung to me and wavered in and out of consciousness. She dug her nails into my palms. There was more blood. Another hour passed, and her face went ghostly white. The sweat on her forehead disappeared. She looked like a corpse, and her breathing grew shallower and weaker. But then she suddenly opened her eyes and looked at me. I'll never forget that stare.

Her face was a strange mixture of shock and joy.

I looked down. The baby's head was coming out.

Kim gasped in agony.

"You're doing great! The baby's coming! Just one more push! You can do it!" I yelled.

But the baby's face was turning blue. I had no idea what I was doing, but I put my fingers around the baby's neck and tried to ease the little body out.

My wife cried out. She looked as if she couldn't bear it a moment longer. I burned with guilt and shame. I couldn't give her a decent life. But I couldn't let her or the baby die.

As I kneeled there, not knowing what I was doing and trying to keep my wife and baby alive, I kept hearing the voices of those bastards from the League back in Japan. *Paradise on earth . . . You'll be happy there . . . Free from poverty at last . . . Independent.* And I thought, *Why should we die in agony in this hellhole of a place? Forget that! We can't let those bastards win.*

I whispered into my wife's ear, "If you die now, it will have been for nothing. Stay with me, and let's beat the lot of them!"

My wife bore down one last time. She let out a blood-curdling cry that seemed to come from the depths of the universe. And then, to my total surprise, the baby slid out in one swift motion.

Kim lay back, utterly spent.

I cut the umbilical cord and wrapped the baby in the ancient rag I'd found. I waited for him to start crying, but he didn't.

"Please cry! Please!" I shouted. And then he did! I guess my loud voice startled him.

Once my wife heard the baby crying, she passed out. I put the baby next to her and dashed from the house. Our nearest neighbor lived about five hundred yards away. I raced over and banged on the door. The woman who lived there was shocked to see me covered with blood, but once I had explained the situation, she rushed out to help. When she entered our house, she stared at the scene in horror and started to cry.

"I've never seen anything so sad in all my life!" she said.

There was blood everywhere. The floor was awash with it. And all we could hear was the sound of the baby crying.

I asked the woman to watch my wife and baby while I ran to the clinic. I banged on the door and woke the doctor up. It was the man I'd beaten up so many years before, but I swallowed my pride, got down on all fours, and lowered my head to the ground.

"It's very serious. My wife and our baby are in life-threatening danger. Please come with me," I begged.

He didn't say anything. Just turned and went back into the clinic. My heart sank. I might have known he would blow me off again.

But then I heard him say, "Let's go."

He emerged from the clinic, and we ran through the dark to my house.

When we arrived, he turned to me in horror.

"You have to get her to the hospital. Now."

I carried her to the hospital on my back while the neighbor stayed with the baby. If anyone had tried to turn me away, I think I would have killed them. But the wardens could see the seriousness of the situation. Or the look in my eyes. They let me in, and I laid my wife on a bed. The dawn's light began to filter through the darkness. The ward faced east, and sunlight soon streamed in through the windows. I'd watched the sunrise the previous morning, but a million years seemed to have passed since then.

I named the baby Ho-son. My wife had given him the gift of life, so I felt it was my mission to look after the baby's health. But my wife was malnourished. She couldn't feed Ho-son herself as she was still recovering in the hospital, so I had to ask around the village whether someone could breast-feed him, just as I had asked when my first son was a baby.

I made daily inquiries around the village, but people were very cold. In a way, I couldn't blame them. The food situation was dire—far worse than when Ho-chol was born. People's kindness had been ground out of them. They were struggling to survive themselves.

I nonetheless continued to beg on his behalf. But they didn't listen. Some even swore at me. But the worst moment was when someone said, "Are you kidding me? You think I care if your baby lives or dies?"

Kim was released from the hospital after a month, but she was still in very poor condition. She couldn't breast-feed Ho-son properly, so he cried all the time. The rickety shack I'd built in Hamju was cold and inhospitable, so I asked my father if my family could stay with him in Dong Chong-ri. Then I swallowed my pride and submitted an application to the central party. Ever since fire destroyed our first house in

1964, I'd never lived in a state-owned property. Although the government was supposed to provide all workers with a house or apartment, there were so many people looking for places and so few places available that you didn't stand a chance of getting one unless you had close links to the party.

Still, I gave it a shot. I explained in my application that I was married but couldn't live with my wife and family because I worked a long way from our home. We desperately needed a place to live. Blah blah blah. I didn't think much would come of it, but six months later, a man came from the housing department to assess my situation. At first I thought that meant we might have a chance. But as usual, my hopes were soon dashed.

After looking around, the man turned to me and said pompously, "You've submitted the correct documents for obtaining accommodation, but why didn't you submit them to the rural district office? Why did you send them to the central party? You've insulted us and wasted my time. Don't you know your place? Behave yourself!"

Behave yourself? I couldn't believe my ears. Did he think I was a child? But I had to be careful. I couldn't take any chances by insulting the party. I apologized meekly and felt that familiar swell of despair.

I couldn't put a proper roof over my family's heads, I would not be able to keep my job, and I wouldn't ever be able to lead a decent life. But shortly after that, I heard that a tractor driver was needed in the forestry-machine factory in Hamhung. I told them I had a tractor driver's license and somehow got the job. It was strictly off the record since, officially speaking, the job didn't exist, but I didn't care.

Hamhung is an industrial city with terrible pollution and the most appalling smog I'd ever seen. The factory I went to work in had apartments for its workers, but there weren't any vacancies. Not that it would have made any difference if there had been since my job was off the record. How would they have accounted for my family in their paperwork?

After staying with my father for a while in Dong Chong-ri, my wife and the younger children went to live with her parents in Hamju. Ho-chol stayed with my father. I hated that we were all split up, but we had no other options. It seemed to me that, whatever I did, I always let my family down. I just wanted us all to live happily together.

I decided to commandeer a room in the factory in Hamhung without permission. When dinnertime came around, I made sure there was no one about, and I took some fuel from the tractor. I used it to cook rice on an oil stove. *Juche* in action again. Autonomy, independence, self-sufficiency. It kept me alive, but it was a miserable existence. Sometimes, I felt so lonely at night that I sobbed like a child.

One Thursday, there was a power outage. This was a regular occurrence, and Thursday had become a kind of unofficial day off. This particular Thursday, I lay on my futon dozing when someone started hammering on my door.

"Are you there?"

I leaped up and opened the door. One of my colleagues who knew where I was hiding was standing there. It turned out the police had been in touch with the factory. Something to do with Ho-chol.

I ran to the police station in Hamhung—and there he was, sitting on a chair with his head bowed. As soon as he saw me, he rushed up to hug me.

He'd been on his way to school, but for some reason, he really wanted to see me, so he'd hopped on a train without buying a ticket. When he got off at Hamhung, he didn't know where to find me, so he ended up wandering about aimlessly. He reminded me of my younger self, so many years ago, searching the streets for my mother in Tokyo. Thieves had assaulted him and stripped him of his shoes and clothes and left him sprawled on the ground, practically naked.

He couldn't stop crying.

"Don't cry! You're a man! You need to be strong!" I said, but inside I ached for him.

I gave him my jacket and took him back to my father's house in Dong Chong-ri.

I got to know a man who managed an electric lightbulb factory in Hamhung City who offered me a job as a driver—off the record, of course. He said if I accepted his offer, he could fix me up with a place to live. I hauled myself over to the factory that very day. I moved in with two single men who worked in the factory. It wasn't my own place, but things seemed to be improving. The manager promised he'd fix up a place for me by the coming winter.

He said I was an "outstanding worker." I don't think I was outstanding at all—just average—but that was enough. But that's the thing. People in North Korea spend so much time in study meetings and calculating the number of hours they've worked that there's no time to *do* the actual work. The result? Raw materials don't arrive in factories, the electricity doesn't work, and farms are overrun with weeds. But as long as people can get their food rations, they don't care. Since my job was off the record, I had no study meetings and was not forced to put in countless hours for pointless bureaucracy. So I could work properly. Or normally, as an ordinary, average worker, as I saw it. But in the manager's eyes, I was outstanding.

It had been a year and a half since my family was split up. But I was pleased to think I would soon secure a place in Hamhung City where my wife and I and our children could all live together again. I put everything into my work.

Several months later, it came time to distribute the Chinese cabbage rations. In winter, each workplace received a supply of Chinese cabbages for the "winter storage battle." Given how hard it was to survive the winter in North Korea, "battle" was an appropriate term.

If you were important to the party, you got more than everyone else. But if you were a factory worker, the number of cabbages you got depended on the size of your family. My job was to label the cabbages with the names of the people they were destined for. I finished the job as quickly as I could and went into the office.

"You told me that you would have a place for me by winter. It's now winter," I said to the manager.

"I just said I'd think about it," he said. "I didn't make any promises."

Think about it? That's not what he'd led me to believe before.

He looked very awkward and uncomfortable, and started scrutinizing his paperwork.

I figured it was pointless to start a fight, and turned to walk away. But then I noticed my muddy hands. Handling all the Chinese cabbages had made them filthy. Suddenly incensed, I turned back. "Do you actually enjoy screwing people over?" I asked.

I grabbed him by the collar and hauled him out of his office. Some workers tried to hold me back, but I couldn't control my anger. We both went flying headfirst into the cabbages.

The next day, the manager came up to me. "Use the room next to the development section," he said bluntly.

It was little more than a shack. It had no kitchen and was constantly throbbing with the din of machines. Even so, I was happy to have a place in Hamhung City to bring my family, so I started making a Korean stove under the floor and cobbled together a kitchen range.

After a few days, it was just about habitable, so I asked my wife and three children to move in. It was small and noisy, but at least we would be together. By this time, Ho-chol was beyond school age and spent his days looking for work. Myong-hwa was in junior high, and Ho-son was in elementary school.

The factory recycled glass bottles and turned them into lightbulbs. But some of the bottles were colored and couldn't be recycled, so I'd take them back home and use them to decorate the place. I viewed them as our treasure.

My factory and another factory decided to band together to build a five-floor apartment block. I knew there was some sort of manager on the project, but he wasn't a professional engineer. We'd all heard the stories. Apartments would be built, winter would come, and the buildings would fall apart come spring due to inferior cement, improper steel frames, and winter temperatures way below zero. When I heard of this building project and its dodgy manager, I naturally had my doubts. But I still envied the people who'd get to live there. I didn't know who'd get selected, but I knew it wouldn't be me.

Except a miracle happened. An acquaintance somehow managed to secure a proper apartment for us. We were over the moon at our good fortune.

Then I had another stroke of luck. One of the managers in the other factory sought me out. "I think we could help each other. There's this job I need done. I can't pay you for it, but if you'd be prepared to take it on, I can help you fix up your place," he said.

The manager was true to his word. He installed a Korean stove under the floor and came up with a decent door and produced some pieces of furniture.

Our apartment was on the fourth floor. We had a toilet and a proper kitchen—luxuries beyond belief. It was the first time I'd lived in a normal place since my family's house had gone up in flames; it was the first time my children had ever had a home of their own.

By the eighties, things had actually changed for the better for returnees. Returnees regularly received money from their relatives back in Japan, and a chosen few could even visit them. A chosen few, mind you. They were called members of "homeland delegations." I could never quite work out which homeland was being referred to, or how these people were chosen, and there was no chance of entire families visiting relatives, of course. Who would ever have returned to North Korea if they had all their loved ones with them? Those who got to leave for visits returned with hard currency and everyday products that were the height of luxury in the impoverished hellhole that was North Korea. As returnees grew wealthier, the party's attitude toward them changed. In the old days, if returnees said the slightest thing wrong, they'd be purged or whisked off to a concentration camp. Now they were considered a positive asset, so the party started treating them better. A canny move, it turned out. There were ways of using hostages.

The black market was also thriving. It seemed the more messed up a country became, the more the black market prospered. If you were lucky enough to have money coming in from Japan, you could get rice or meat. It would cost you ten times the official rate, but that didn't matter if you had access to foreign currency. Yesterday, you were scraping along at rock bottom, a social pariah, but now you had members of the party over for dinner. Yesterday, you were just another "hostile." Today, you were welcomed into the fold.

But we were in no position to enjoy that kind of good fortune. Our relatives in Japan had cut us off. Our fellow returnees mocked us and despised us, wanted nothing to do with us. I could hardly bear the hypocrisy of it. I was scrabbling for whatever work I could find to make some kind of living, while they sponged off their relatives and reveled in their unearned new status.

My children were old enough to be aware of the discrepancy between what we had and what others had. One day, one of them asked, "Dad, why don't we have any nice things? All the other returnees have fridges and televisions. They get all sorts of gifts from their relatives in Japan. I thought you said our grandfather did great things in Japan." What broke my heart more than anything else was that they weren't allowed to do taekwondo like their classmates, because I couldn't afford the correct uniforms for them. So they just sat there, at the edge of the room, watching the other kids participate. It wasn't even my children who told me this; I heard about it from their classmates' parents. Myong-hwa and Ho-son knew better than to ask me to buy them uniforms. So they tried to spare me the pain and humiliation by not bringing up the subject.

In the autumn of 1984, I found a new job, this time in a food-distribution center. Products from various factories were collected here and were then driven to delivery points in each district. The prices, fixed by the government, were the same all over the country. The amount delivered depended on the size of the local population.

One of my coworkers there eventually hooked me up with a job in soybean paste and soy sauce distribution. Any kind of job connected with food was a ticket to a better life. Not only did it give you access to food for your family, but it also gave you access to party bigwigs. If you played your cards right and sent enough goodies their way, you could get televisions or fridges or other perks in return. In the West, I guess you'd call it corruption. In North Korea, it was just standard operating procedure. Suddenly I had access to soybean paste and soy sauce. There was no way I would let such an opportunity pass me by.

When I delivered soybean paste and soy sauce to nearby villages, I couldn't help but notice how thin and tired the local farmers looked. They all had the same pinched and starving appearance. Their food ration was supposed to be one and a half pounds a day, but they only received about half that amount. It didn't help that they were constantly being called away from their work for military training or other urgent projects. Because they were unable to attend to their land, everything went to wrack and ruin. I saw countless farms overrun with weeds simply because the farmers had no time to look after them.

Around this time, a rift developed between Ho-chol and his stepmother. Adolescent sons and their stepmothers don't get along; it seems to be a law of nature. He'd hit puberty and become volatile. My wife had also grown more distant and withdrawn from her own children and seemed to be shrinking into herself. Ho-chol returned to my village, Dong Chong-ri, to live with my father for a while. I asked my boss to find him a position in the Hamju area—food-storage work, anything that would keep him from being consigned to the thankless toil of being a farm laborer, which would be his only option if he stayed in Dong Chong-ri. In a rare stroke of luck, my boss managed to get Ho-chol a job.

On Ho-chol's seventeenth birthday, March 25, 1989, I lied to my wife. I told her I was going to work, but when I left the house, I picked up some bread and went to visit my son. I hadn't seen him for two months, and he looked more mature than before. We went to the river and had lunch together. We shared the corn rice and bread that I'd brought. It was hardly a birthday feast, but it tasted good.

We enjoyed chatting, but when we got to talking about the past and everything we'd been through, I couldn't help but weep. He tried to comfort me but ended up crying himself. He was always an empathic child, and as he grew into a man, he was one of the few people in the world who I felt truly understood me. I tried to give him some advice.

"Grow up. Get married and learn to stand on your own two feet, because I have absolutely no idea what's going to happen to me. If you're sick, if you need help, just tell me, okay? I'll always do whatever I can for you."

We shook hands firmly and separated.

Only a few days later, a policeman summoned me. He claimed that my son had stolen a goat, and he wanted me to pay for it. I immediately went to my son's place to find out what was going on.

When I found him, I saw that he had bruises all over his face.

"I haven't done anything wrong. I've been framed," he said.

He explained there were about forty workers in his workplace; he was the youngest. Some bad apples who worked there had stolen some potatoes and sweet corn from the village storage shed. Worse still, they'd killed some domestic animals and eaten them. Then they'd blamed everything on my son.

"They told me, 'You're a returnee and very young, so you'll be treated with more lenience. So you need to take the blame for everything, okay?' I didn't feel like I had a choice." His voice trembled.

And then Ho-chol told me they'd beaten him up.

I looked at my son. I knew he hadn't done anything wrong. The sight of his bruises broke my heart.

"Listen! You have to be strong and brave! You have to learn how to fight your own battles if you want to survive," I said.

I left feeling very worried. As soon as I got home, the police started badgering me again. They claimed that if I didn't pay compensation, my son would be sent to a concentration camp. I felt sick to my stomach. I absolutely couldn't let that happen.

I got the idea of trying to get him into the military as a last resort. At least it would remove him from his current mess. So I went to the local recruitment center and said my son was eager to join up. I even offered them some soybean paste and soy sauce to sweeten the deal.

Though they initially said no, I didn't give up that easily. I went back every day after work. Oh, I knew my chances of success were slim, but what did I have to lose? If my son couldn't enter the military, he'd be arrested. He'd disappear. I was desperate.

They eventually threw me out of the recruitment center. So my hopes, yet again, were at an end.

The following day, I went to see Ho-chol. I'd decided to take him back home with me to Hamhung City. I told him how I'd tried to get him signed up at the recruitment center, but to no avail. His best chance would be to get away for a while and lie low until they forgot about him.

Some young men wearing military uniforms stood in front of the station as we waited to board the train. They were new recruits, smiling and holding hands with their parents, looking very content with themselves. Some of them were taking souvenir photographs. I could picture the inscription, THE DAY OUR SON JOINED THE MILITARY. A happy memory.

My son began to weep, but not tears of joy. The sight of him brought tears to my eyes as well. "Father! Please don't cry too! You've done so much for me ever since I was born. I know that, and people in the village have told me as well. You've made it through so many hard times; I know you did everything you could."

At that, I broke down completely. I hugged him and started sobbing loudly, even though the station was full of people.

The new recruits started walking proudly onto the platform. Suddenly, I had an idea. I told my son to get on the same train. I thought that maybe he could get swept along with them and end up in training with them. It also struck me that I might never see him again. I wanted to take a photograph with him, but of course that was impossible.

I gave him ten won. It was all I had.

"Look after yourself. I think the police will forget about you after a while, so try to make the best of it until then," I said.

"Don't worry, Father. I'll contact you when I can. I'll definitely come back and find you."

He boarded the train. The doors slammed. A desolate whistle sounded. Then the train started to move.

I looked at my son, but I couldn't see him properly. Hot tears blurred my vision.

I kept waving until the train was out of sight.

After my son's departure, I worried that I might go off the rails, so I asked my father and sister if we could come and live with them in Dong Chong-ri. Technically, citizens had no freedom of movement. But since we'd dropped out of the system, we could move about without the police getting involved. They only very rarely came after people like us; usually they just couldn't be bothered.

So we moved back in with my father and sister Masako. We were nicknamed "the Penniless Returnees." Myong-hwa and Ho-son missed their older brother terribly. I could tell they worried about him, even though they tried to keep such thoughts to themselves. Ho-chol had always looked after them, like another parent, from the time they were babies. They obviously felt his absence acutely; it made my own pain in missing him even worse.

One day, when my father was alone at home, a young man knocked on the door. My father immediately recognized him as one of the hoodlums who hung around on the street.

"Sell this to a rich returnee! If you sell it, you can keep some of the profit," he said to my father.

And what *was* this wonderful item that he waved in front of my father's face? A seal penis, I kid you not. It was apparently something greatly valued in Chinese medicine. Any kind of medicine was hard to come by in North Korea, so something like that would command a high price. The thug shoved the penis into my father's hand and ran off before he could answer.

My father smelled a rat. We were known for being poor; the thug must have known that. So what was he hoping to get out of us? Why didn't the punk just sell it himself? Why lose a share of the profit? But in the end, my father thought, "Well, if I can make some money out of it . . ."

It proved to be a fatal mistake.

He went off looking for a buyer, and before he knew it, the penis was snatched away by another thug. Although my father was seventy-four years old, he still had a young man's mind. So what did he do?

He tried to chase after his assailant. But his legs just weren't up to it anymore.

"Thief! Thief! Stop thief!" he shouted.

No one paid him any attention. Things like that happened all the time in North Korea. My father lost sight of the man and returned home.

That night, the first thug came back to our house.

"I've found someone who wants to buy that seal penis. I need it back," he said.

"Do you think I was born yesterday? Do you think I can't recognize a scam when it's staring me in the face?" I said.

"If you dare to make a false accusation against me, I'll beat the living daylights out of you, you piece of shit."

"You know where you can shove that seal penis of yours?" I slammed the door in his face.

He left, but he kept coming back. Day after day. If I wasn't around, he beat up my father and sister. Then the police summoned my father. When he returned after midnight, his face was black and blue. The inside of his mouth was cut and his lips were bloodstained.

Some tough young cop had beaten him up. He kept going on about the seal penis. "Where is it, you bastard? This is North Korea. You don't mess with the law. This is what it feels like if you mess with the law."

And so the beating resumed. In the past, my father had been known for his ability to defend himself, but this was a different time and place. There was nothing he could say or do. I was helpless as well. I was furious that this thug had taken advantage of him like that, but I knew the police would never listen. There was just no way around the corruption.

My father never truly recovered from that brutal beating. As he grew weaker, I kept picturing him as he had once been back in Japan. The Tiger. Brawny beyond belief. By 1994, he couldn't stand up on his own, and he spent his days in bed. Soon, he couldn't even stomach the thinnest gruel.

One day, he called us all to his bedside. "I'm dying," he said. "But you have to stay alive. You have to get back to Japan. One way or another, you must. And when you get back, let everyone know I'm dead. My old friends will help you out." My children cried and called out to him, "Grandpa! Grandpa!"

I was desperate to get my hands on some medicine for him, but we didn't have any money. He deteriorated quickly. Soon he found it difficult to breathe, and shortly after that he stopped speaking.

One afternoon, he beckoned me over. When I went over to him, he tried to speak, but I couldn't understand. I eventually grasped that he wanted the tiny hoe that my mother used to use to dig up root vegetables and mountain weeds. I had no idea what he wanted it for, but you don't deny a dying man.

As soon as I gave it to him, he tried to shove it down his throat.

I grabbed it away from him. "What the hell are you doing?" I yelled.

He pointed to his throat. It was blocked with phlegm, and he was struggling to breathe.

His breathing grew shallower. My son and daughter rubbed his arms and legs in an effort to help his circulation.

After a while, he looked up at me with his eyes open wide. I'll never forget that stare. He opened his mouth to speak, but all his strength had gone. All we could hear was the sound of his labored breathing. Then he closed his eyes.

He snored for twenty minutes or so, and I let myself think he just might pull through.

But then the snoring stopped. The room fell silent. The man known as Tiger was dead.

I buried him on the far side of the mountain in Dong Chong-ri, facing south toward the sea. That way he could see South Korea, his mother country. His funeral was a perfunctory affair in the administration office of the factory where I worked. I didn't know where Eiko was, so I couldn't even tell her of our father's death. I sent Hifumi a telegram, but she didn't arrive in time. My father had so many friends over the course of his life and had helped so many people along the way, but not one of them was there to lay him to rest.

I still don't know what my father made of his wreck of a life. I never will. He knew he'd been deceived by the League, but he never really complained about his lot. Did he feel some kind of misguided patriotism through it all? I'll never know. I loved him, of course, but there are things I will never understand about him.

Sometime after his death, my sister Masako informed my wife and me that she'd found a job, and she moved out with her two stepchildren. I didn't know what kind of job she could possibly have found, since there weren't any jobs to be had, but she may have left simply because there wasn't enough food to go around. I felt very empty and alone after they left.

A few weeks later, her stepkids burst into our house in the middle of the night. Their mother was being beaten up by a whole group of people, they yelled frantically. I had to do something.

They led me through the icy streets to the place where they were staying. Five young men sat in a pitch-black room, surrounding my sister.

One man was trying to block the entrance. "Are you her brother? I lent her ten thousand yen. If you can't pay me back, I'm going to kill the bitch," he said in a very low voice.

"What the hell kind of person are you? Beating her up right in front of her children. You'll get your money back. I'll see to it. Now, piss off before I break your neck!" I yelled.

He hesitated, and I knew he was sizing me up, trying to decide if he and his cronies should come after me as well. But he just clenched his fists, called off his men, and vanished.

I found a light switch by the door and flipped it, but there was no electricity.

My sister was sobbing. Her stepchildren burst into tears and hugged her. I peered around the room. It was difficult to see much in the darkness, but one thing was obvious: there wasn't a single stick of furniture in it. They were clearly squatting there. And the job she'd talked about? Obviously a fabrication. No job meant no food ration. All she could do to survive was borrow money.

But ten thousand yen! It was only the equivalent of eighty dollars or so, but to me, that was an astronomical sum. Even if you had a proper job, it would take several years to save up that amount. What had she done with it?

I tried to borrow some money to help her, but it was hopeless. I asked everyone I could think of. Returnees. Managers in the factory. Even people who'd previously looked down on me. But everyone was struggling to survive themselves.

I eventually decided to visit Ro Jegu-an. We'd attended the same Korean school in Yokohama, and he was the richest returnee in Hamhung. I didn't really think he'd remember me, but he was our only chance. So I looked him up.

When I arrived at his place, I just stared at the doorknob, which was so polished that I could see my reflection in its gleaming surface. I found myself wiping my hands on my work pants and straightening my clothes—not that it mattered. When I looked down at my shoes, I saw that my big toes were poking out, and my tattered shirt was missing some buttons. I suddenly felt ashamed of myself, but I had no choice. I took a deep breath and knocked on the door.

"Who is it?" Then the door opened, and a man's face appeared. He had a round face and rosy cheeks. He was the picture of health.

I kind of jammed myself in the doorway so that he couldn't just slam the door in my face.

"My name's Masaji Ishikawa. I don't suppose you remember me, but we went to the same school in Yokohama. I think we may have spoken once or twice. The fact is, I've come here to ask you a favor."

He looked suspicious. "I'm sorry. I don't remember you. It was such a long time ago. Anyway, you'd better come in."

The whole experience was surreal. I'd never seen anything like his place. My eyes moved from the TV to the telephone to the sparkling chandelier to the furnishings fit for a queen and then down to the sumptuous carpet. It felt soft beneath my big toes. And room after room after room. The place seemed to go on forever. I could hardly take it all in.

I sat down across from him on the sofa. His wife brought a cup of tea and put it on the low table in front of me. I lowered my head. There was some expensive-looking candy on a small silver tray. Why on earth do I remember that? I don't know. But I do remember I told him the truth about my sister, about how desperate our situation had become. I asked if he could lend me some money. I promised to pay him back.

He coughed once and then fell silent. I waited, trying to think how to fill the painful silence.

Finally he said, "Hold your head up! Don't sit bowed down like that!"

He turned to his wife and asked her something, his voice very low. I have no idea what he said, but his wife looked very cross and made no attempt to hide her irritation.

Then a miracle happened. Ten thousand yen appeared, right there on the table in front of me. I could scarcely believe my eyes. I could pay back my sister's debt in its entirety! I forced back my tears and thanked the man from the bottom of my heart as best I could. I couldn't find the words, and my throat felt constricted, like I could barely breathe. I was overwhelmed with gratitude and relief as I left his sumptuous home.

As usual, however, I was too optimistic. Oh sure, I paid off my sister's debt, but a few days later, she simply disappeared. It turned out she'd borrowed money from other people too. I have no idea what she spent that money on. I'll be wondering about that till the day I die.

I heard rumors occasionally. They were seen sleeping near the station. Then they were sleeping in front of someone's house, living on whatever scraps they could find on the street. I went looking for them whenever I heard news of where they might be, but I could never find them. I never saw them again.

CHAPTER 5

July 8, 1994, began like any other day. The sky above Hamhung was thick with haze. You would have thought a storm was on the way, but the billowing clouds were actually just smoke from the factories.

I went to work as usual. Around lunchtime, a woman's high-pitched voice came across the factory speakers, announcing that we should be prepared for a special news bulletin. I couldn't imagine what it could be.

I was taking a break, standing in a corner and smoking a cigarette, when solemn music suddenly started booming from the speaker above my head.

"There is very important news. There is very important news. Today, the Great Leader, Comrade Kim Il-sung, passed away!"

The factory abruptly fell silent. Everyone stopped what they were doing and stood there dumbfounded. But not for long. Soon a great clamor filled the air. People began crying and wailing, while others pounded the workbenches and walls.

My cigarette slipped from my fingers, and my jaw dropped. To my utter shock, I found myself crying too. I have no idea why, but hot tears streamed down my cheeks. Was it shock? Fear? Relief? I felt a strange mixture of feelings that I've never been able to explain to this day.

I'd spent more than thirty years living in this "paradise on earth" created by Kim Il-sung; I'd been treated as little more than an animal and barely survived at the very bottom rung of society. At one point,

I'd even tried to end my life to escape my miserable existence here. So why was I crying?

Had all of the state programming been partially successful? Ever since moving to North Korea, I'd never felt truly alive; part of me had been walled off, silenced. After a while, I felt that that part of me had simply withered away like a limb that atrophies from lack of use. I pondered the terror that had dominated my life—the never-ending surveillance; the lack of autonomy; the fear of expressing an opinion; the hopelessness and despair; the impossibility of improving my lot in life. Kim Il-sung's menacing rule had invaded every single aspect of my life, like a bayonet inches from my throat.

I'd been saying, "Long live Kim Il-sung!" for more than thirty years—not ever meaning it, of course—but here I was crying. Had all the brainwashing achieved its desired effect? Or was I just responding to group hysteria? The people around me were completely distraught. "How are we going to live from now on?" they kept wailing.

When I got home, my children clung to me and cried. My wife wept too. I don't know whether any of it was from sadness, or whether it was all rooted in fear. What would happen to us now?

The day after his death, people flocked to his bronze statue and placed flowers before it. Cinemas and cultural facilities hosted memorial gatherings. Attendance was compulsory. The police were everywhere, just to make sure that everyone turned up. But it wasn't necessary. Everyone was eager to attend, to share their feelings with others, to feel a part of something larger and more meaningful than their own pitiful little lives.

Kim Il-sung died on the eve of what was supposed to have been the first ever North-South Summit. The party leadership had been delirious with optimism about the summit, claiming that the unification of

North and South would soon become a reality and that our present difficulties would be over.

But that's the trouble with propaganda. It constantly contradicts itself. We had been told that the collapse of farming and the demise of the economy were entirely the fault of US imperialists dividing the Korean Peninsula into two countries. If only the North and South could be unified, the threat of starvation would be over.

But that didn't make any sense. If our troubles were purely the result of US imperialism, why weren't South Koreans starving too? And besides, only the other day, hadn't we been told that they *were* starving too? In that case, how would the unification save us?

As time went on, workers in the factory all began to ask the same question: How are we supposed to live now that the Great Leader is dead? I don't think they were prompted by sorrow. The question was prompted by fear. You could see it in their faces. They were terrified. As well they might be. Starvation was staring us all in the face. Never mind that there was a sumptuous ceremony to celebrate Kim Jong-il's inauguration as the new Great Leader.

As soon as Kim Jong-il took over, people began to complain about him. They blamed him for the deteriorating food situation. They were secretly contemptuous of him, saying he had become the country's leader only because of his father. True enough. When Kim Il-sung was still alive, the propaganda machine had been cranked up to the limit. Kim Il-sung, the Great Leader, peace be upon him, had liberated the people from the yoke of tyranny. More or less single-handedly. Why wouldn't they trust and respect him? "This is the year of agriculture," he announced in 1992. "The nation must realize the people's century-long dream to eat white rice and meat soup, wear silken clothes, and live in tiled-roof homes."

Trouble was, I'd heard it all before. The very same speech. Way back in 1961. Not long after I'd moved to North Korea. The very same idiotic speech! The same shameless lavish self-praise. But Kim Il-sung had never fulfilled any of his promises. Not one. He promised us "paradise on earth" and instead consigned us to its very opposite.

When I think of all the people he purged, all the people he starved, all the incalculable suffering he caused, I have to hope that his name goes down in infamy.

Ever since setting foot in North Korea more than thirty years before, I'd known nothing but hunger. Everyone had been halfway to starvation for decades. But things had taken a turn for the worse starting in 1991. From 1991 until Kim Il-sung's death in 1994, extremely cold weather wreaked havoc on the fragile food supply.

Under the food-distribution system, regular workers were officially entitled to one and a half pounds of grain per day. For some perverse reason, farmers were entitled to less than that. The actual amount, even for regular workers, was one pound, 70 percent of which was just cornstarch. Needless to say, party members received a much larger ration.

Rations were supposed to be distributed twice a month, but beginning in 1991, there were regular delays. In the end, we had to survive for half a month on three days' worth of food. Inevitably, things turned nasty. People descended on the food-distribution stations, and violence broke out in explosive bursts.

The party started churning out more slogans, more propaganda. I couldn't help but wonder where they even got all the paper for the posters—and whether I could eat it. And what did all these wretched posters tell us? They gave advice on alternatives to the standard food ration.

"Make the root of rice plants into a powder and eat it! It's rich in protein! . . . Arrowroot contains a lot of starch! . . . If you eat and survive, we can definitely prevail!" Useless information, all delivered with the usual histrionic exclamation marks. By that time, we'd been scouring the ground for ages for anything edible—acorns, mugwort, pine-tree bark. It was hellish stuff. You can use bark to make something vaguely resembling a rice cake. It was a dreadful thing. People had eaten it out of desperation at the end of the colonial era and again just after the Korean War. Times when people had no other choice. Times like the ones we found ourselves in.

Here's how to make it. First, boil the pine bark for as long as possible to get rid of all the toxins. (Many people botched this stage and died in agony as a result.) Next, add some cornstarch and steam the evil brew. Then cool it, form it into cakes, and eat it. This was easier said than done. The pine oil stinks to high heaven and makes it almost impossible to consume it. But if you wanted to live, you choked it down.

That's when the real fun began. Crippling gut pain that brought us to our knees; constipation that you wouldn't believe. When the pain became unbearable—there's no delicate way of putting this—you had to shove your finger up your anus and scoop out your concrete shit. I'm sorry. You didn't need to know that. Except you did. It's the only thing that shows how desperate we were.

After the death of Kim Il-sung, everything ground to a halt. Farming. Industry. Everything. No raw materials of any kind got delivered to the factory. We had only a few hours of electricity, if we were lucky. Production gradually sputtered out. Workers collapsed on the floor before my eyes, weak with hunger.

Sometimes we received an official notice from the party, giving us permission to cultivate any vacant land we could find. So we'd grab our shovels and find a strip of land by the roadside or up against an apartment building. We'd hoe the soil and plant beans or Chinese cabbages. Others created plots on mountainsides and attempted to plant sweet corn and potatoes. But it was a waste of effort. It was almost impossible to find seeds, and even if you did manage to find some and get something to grow, it would be stolen before the harvest. The crops were pulled when they were no bigger than your thumb.

Children gave up going to school. I'd see them wandering the streets with the adults, desperately searching for food. Myong-hwa and Ho-son got thinner and thinner, their faces so sunken that their eyes looked huge, entirely out of proportion to their other features. I wanted to cry whenever I looked at their small bony bodies, but I lacked even the energy for that.

The situation grew more and more dire. Starving people wandered around hopelessly, while others simply lay in the street. Soon there were corpses too, lying out in the open, unclaimed and left to rot. Women. Old people. Kids.

The black market operated openly. Stalls sprang up right in front of the police station, and the authorities couldn't do anything about it. Not the cops, not even the dreaded secret police. If they'd tried to intervene, all hell would have broken loose.

Not that the black market was any use to people who didn't have hard currency. If you tried to buy something with local currency, the price went up a hundredfold unless you had a watch or some useful household items to barter.

Someone like me—with no hard currency and no goods to exchange—could only buy rice gruel from a shop that a cockroach would have fled from. That, or wander about the market in hopes of picking up some crumbs another unlucky bastard had inadvertently dropped.

The only other option was to steal. That was the quickest and easiest solution, and it grew increasingly common.

Another huge change that occurred around this time was that it suddenly became much easier to move around. In the past, you couldn't get on a train without official travel documents. But now you were free to go anywhere if you had a ticket, which usually simply involved bribing someone.

Not that I could take advantage of these changing circumstances, as I had no money. Production at the factory I worked in had gradually ceased, so I had no goods to trade.

My family and I started to pick a plant called *omode*. We searched and picked till it got dark, by which time our hands were bleeding. Once we had a decent bag of it, we returned home and peeled off the skin. Mashed the flesh. Boiled the stuff. It tasted foul, but we'd eat anything to survive.

I sometimes felt ashamed of myself. I worried about Ho-chol; I had no idea where he was, but I thought about him all the time. I apologized to the kids and to my wife for our miserable life. My children were always kind, always hopeful. They knew I liked a smoke whenever I could get my hands on one, so they used to pick up cigarette butts and give them to me. We were on the verge of starvation, but the bonds of family love remained intact. Which was more than you could say for some people. I heard many stories of families falling out over food. I even heard a rumor of one man killing his wife and eating her. I'm sure it was true, and I'm equally sure he wasn't the only one.

By the summer of 1995, we were truly terrified that we might die of hunger. Then in August, disaster struck. A devastating flood hit South Pyongan Province, an important grain-producing area. That meant the end of our grain ration. When autumn came, we started to collect acorns in desperation. With no grain, acorns were the only things that might see us through the coming winter. So we collected as many as we possibly could. We boiled them and ate them once a day, and to us, God help us, they tasted delicious. And yes, they did see us through.

By the spring of 1996, the land we'd cultivated next to our apartment building was useless. There were no young seedlings to plant, no seeds, and no fertilizer either. The factory had shut down. By this time, so many people had died that I saw hordes of orphans wandering around.

It got so bad that we eventually started eating any old weeds we could find. We boiled the wretched things for ages to try to get rid of their harshness. But it was hopeless. They still tasted rank. And they did the most appalling things to us. Our bodies grew swollen, our faces grew swollen, and our urine turned red or even blue. We all suffered from chronic diarrhea. We couldn't even walk in that condition.

No one thought or talked about anything except food. When we could manage to get around, we spent all our time searching and searching for anything remotely edible. We were nothing but a bunch of ravenous ghosts. The barely living dead.

I don't know how many people starved to death. You heard stories all the time.

"That woman whose husband died? Well, she's dead too. Died alone."

"I haven't seen old so-and-so recently. Have *you*? I guess he didn't make it."

"I found this woman lying on the street. I checked, but she was cold already."

I heard stories of cannibalism. Rumor had it that if those participating in such acts got caught, they were executed in public. I never witnessed a public execution myself, but it wouldn't surprise me. Every day was like living in a nightmare. It sounds dreadful to say, but I grew immune to the horror of all the people lying in the streets. Sometimes, I couldn't tell whether they were dying or already dead. And the awful thing was, I didn't have the energy to care.

People started asking awkward questions in public. Like, when would they be able to eat white rice and meat soup? No one would have asked a question like that in the past, not even in private.

Some people complained about Kim Il-sung and what he'd gotten us into. But nobody spoke of changing the system. They were too scared of the police and the secret police. Did anyone even try to topple the leadership? No. They did what they were told to the bitter end. After all, they'd been brainwashed since they were schoolchildren. We were taught that the United States brutally slaughters our brothers and sisters in the south. That we must free the people of South Korea. That their country is occupied by the enemy, the United States.

I wasn't sure how my family and I survived. We all had the same sunken eyes and hollow cheeks, bodies of skin and bone. When we sat or lay down, we were so bony, it hurt. Even when we were sleeping, it was so painful, we woke up constantly.

When I looked at my family, I thought, *Dear God! Do we have to die like this?*

I grew reluctant to pick weeds. We were dying anyway. What was the point? I became indifferent to death. If I could just stand the pain and lie down for a while, I could float away and never come back.

But it was always the same. Every time I closed my eyes, I heard my parents' voices, their dying words. I was obsessed with them.

Somehow . . . somehow . . . get back to Japan! Tell our story! my father said.

Take my ashes back to Japan and put them in my parents' grave, my mother's sobbing voice echoed.

It was September, and the moon sometimes appeared between the clouds. The house in Hamju was dark because we had no electricity. There was no conversation between us. We were sitting slumped by the wall, staring out into the darkness. The moonlight was falling on my wife and children. Their bodies looked like trees in that chilly light. Dead trees.

When you're starving to death, you lose all the fat from your lips and nose. Once your lips disappear, your teeth are bared all the time, like a snarling dog. Your nose is reduced to a pair of nostrils. I wish desperately that I didn't know these things, but I do.

I finally spoke.

"We've been reduced to skeletons. If we don't do anything about it, we'll be dead soon. I have to get across the border. I want you to come with me, but I don't think you have the strength . . ." The thought came to me just like that; I'd never even considered it before. But it suddenly occurred to me that if I was going to die anyway, I might as well die trying to get back to Japan. If by some miracle I succeeded, I could send money back to my family. I could save them.

Myong-hwa was silent for a while. "Father, you must decide," she said. Then she burst into tears.

"We'll be all right. As long as we stay alive, we'll find each other again," my wife said.

I stood up immediately and gathered my few things. I knew that if I didn't leave at once, I'd change my mind. So I went to the front door.

"If I manage to get back to Japan, somehow or other, no matter what it takes, I'll get you there too."

I fought back my tears and set off for Hamju Station. I knew there'd be a night train heading for Hyesan near the border. Suddenly I felt strangely free. I'd crossed an invisible threshold, and my life would never be the same again. I'd just left everything I knew and everyone I loved, and there was no going back. I was going to escape, or die trying.

It wasn't easy to get a train to Pyongyang or the border. You needed special travel documents, and they were harder to obtain than ever. There were too many people like me trying to escape to China.

When I got to Hamju Station, there were lots of people hanging around. IDs and tickets were being checked at the ticket barrier. Not good. I walked about two hundred yards away from the station and crossed the railroad.

A high wall and a barrier of plants were there to prevent people from crossing over the platform, but I managed to squeeze in behind the wall as quietly as I could. I must have gotten caught on some barbed wire because my work pants were now torn to pieces and I was bleeding at the knees. I peeked out from behind the wall to check out the situation on the platform.

Lots of people were waiting for the train. Some were sleeping on the ground. Others were eating. There were a few policemen. And lots of soldiers. Of course. The station was also used by the military. Again not good.

I stayed hidden and watched for what felt like several hours. Eventually, the soldiers lined up, and a train pulled into the station. Even in the darkness, I could see that it was old and rusty and that all the glass had been stolen from the window frames.

I was trying to work out the best moment to jump on the train. Should I get on it right now? No. Too risky. Better to wait until the last possible moment. But how would I know when that was?

I dithered so much and time passed so quickly that, before I knew it, the train was moving. I realized that it was now or never. I bent down and sprinted toward the train as fast as my weary body would carry me. I was running flat out, scared out of my wits and convinced that one of the soldiers would shoot me in the back.

I stuck my arms out and grasped for the ladder at the tail end of the carriage. My hands met the metal bar, and I curled my fingers around it and hauled myself up. The force of my action was so powerful, I ended up somersaulting into the carriage.

I found myself lying in the narrow aisle between the seats, faceup. I was out of breath, so exhausted from my effort that I couldn't move. It was very dark. There was no light on the ceiling above me. Eventually, I sat up and looked around. The seats were all taken. Some people were walking down the aisle, but no one seemed to take any notice of me. Loads of people stole rides in those days, so I guess my arrival was no big deal. All around me, people were nodding off.

And suddenly it hit me. I'd done it. I'd actually managed to get on that train. Relief flooded through me. Suddenly I felt hungry. I'd only had a bowl of soup that morning, many hours ago. I sat with my back against the door at the end of the carriage and dozed off. But then suddenly, I became aware of a light coming from the next carriage. Some kind of inspector was checking passengers' travel documents with a flashlight. Suddenly I was wide awake.

I sat in the dark looking on in horror. My pulse was racing again. I knew that it would be the end of me—and my family—if I got caught. My armpits were clammy with sweat. If I didn't think of something fast, everyone in my family would end up in a concentration camp for the rest of their lives. And as for me, I'd be found guilty of treason and shot.

I glanced around, adrenaline pumping through my veins, but there was nowhere to hide. Everything seemed to go silent. All I could hear was my heart pounding and the sound of the wind.

I didn't have time to hesitate.

"Excuse me. I'm sorry," I said to the passengers sleeping on the seat beside me.

Somehow, I managed to squeeze past them and reach the window. The glassless window.

Oh heavenly glass thief! How I could hug you and kiss you right now!

I put my feet on the window frame and climbed up. I stood on the window frame on the outside of the train. The wind bit into the cuts around my knees, and my bony body was nearly blown away. I knew my legs were still visible from inside the train. I had to find a way to climb onto the roof.

When I looked out over the roof, I could see some kind of ventilation grille. It was difficult to make out exactly what it was. But it came to me in a flash that it was something I could grab hold of. It was just barely out of arm's reach. I would have to risk it. All I'd have to do was jump up and grasp it and pull myself up.

All! I'm five foot three!

We were rapidly approaching a bridge. I could make out some blackish trees up ahead.

I closed my eyes and took a slow, deep breath. When the train reached the bridge, there was a sudden jolt.

Now!

I jumped with all the strength I had. And suddenly, I was in midair, the scenery frozen around me. My fingers hooked the grille. I grabbed it and swung my lower body up and levered myself onto my elbows. I'd made it. I was on the roof. I was trembling from the effort and the terror of that jump. It was a long time before I stopped shaking.

I don't know how long I was up there. I was so tense, I didn't even notice when it started to rain. When I finally regained my senses, my shirt was already soaked through. It would soon be very slick on the roof, and I was in danger of falling off.

I got on my stomach and slithered as carefully as I could to the back of the train. I felt another surge of relief flood through me as my feet made contact with the ladder. I climbed down and hid on the coupler. If I wrapped my arms around the ladder and locked my hands together, I'd be safe enough.

The ladder! Why hadn't I used the fucking ladder when I had to climb out of the train in the first place? I'd been sitting on the floor with my back to the door. All I'd needed to do was . . .

Never mind. I made it. That was all that mattered.

Sometime around midnight, the train reached a dark and deserted station. I recognized the name on the worn sign. It was the stop before Hyesan. I decided it was too risky to go all the way into Hyesan. I might get asked for my travel documents at the station, and that would be the end of me. So it was time to part company with the coupler and the ladder. I jumped off the train and walked off into the night. I knew the Yalu River wasn't far away.

The Yalu River separates China and North Korea. A lot of people cross over it, and even more try to. Bizarrely, some thirty years earlier, many

Chinese Koreans and Chinese had tried to escape *to* North Korea during China's "Great Leap Forward" and Cultural Revolution, that country's own attempt at mass starvation. Now the whole migration had been thrown into reverse.

The town of Hyesan is famous for its coalfields and copper mines. About twelve miles northeast of Hyesan, there's an area called Pochonbo, famous for a battle that took place there in 1937. The Koreans were attempting to push the Japanese occupiers out of their country, and the Anti-Japanese Guerrilla Corps, allegedly commanded by Kim Il-sung, beat the daylights out of the Japanese army. Because of that, it became known as "the Holy Land of Revolution." The city has a huge monument to the revolution and a statue of Kim Il-sung.

How things change! By 1996, the Holy Land of Revolution was infamous as a place people holed up when trying to escape to China. It was patrolled twenty-four hours a day by legions of border security guards.

I'd heard some terrible stories about what happened to people caught trying to escape; everyone had. Horrific stories. Who knows if they were true, or if they were just propagated by the state to keep us in our place. One of the worst I'd heard was the "nose-ring case." A family of four had escaped, but the North Korean police caught them in China. The North Korean police pushed a wire through their noses to link them all together. The Chinese customs officers were shocked at such cruelty and explained that such things weren't allowed in China. Irritated by the Chinese officers' judgment, the police, showing off their barbarous power to the Chinese customs officers, shot the whole family as soon as the group stepped back onto North Korean soil.

After hopping off the train, I walked for such a long time that my legs became as stiff as boards. But finally, I got to Hyesan. I hadn't eaten for two days, so I headed for the market. It was huge, and there were so many products, I felt dizzy. Rice . . . flour . . . walleye pollock roe . . . you name it. Some people were clearly shopping for something to buy, while others looked like homeless people, unable to do anything but look on enviously.

I had no money, of course, so I tried to find something on the ground. I eventually spotted some abandoned corncobs. There were no kernels on them, but I fastened my teeth on the cobs and ate what I could.

When I turned around, I saw a small child behind me. All alone. An orphan, I guess. Like me, he was looking for something edible on the ground. And when he found something, he picked it up and ate it. Like a pigeon. I wondered what had become of his parents. I couldn't think too much about it because it brought to mind images of my own children. And I didn't have the energy to weep.

I wanted to recover my strength, such as it was, so I went to a park in the city center. I found a bush and crept under it. I soon fell asleep on the hard ground. In the morning, I got up and walked around in front of the train station for a bit. I got lucky and found an apple core. I started munching on it and headed for the river. By the time I got to the banks, it was nearly midday.

The first thing I felt when I saw the river was surprise. The river was so narrow; it couldn't have been more than about thirty yards wide. If it had been winter and the surface had been frozen, I could have crossed it in a matter of seconds. More than enough time to get shot in the back, mind you, but I tried not to think about that.

I spotted some men standing around talking and smoking cigarettes on the opposite bank—in China. On the North Korean side, there were sentry boxes every fifty yards or so, and guards carrying rifles were on round-the-clock patrol. Some of them had menacing-looking German shepherds by their sides. I spotted a woman washing some clothes in the river and quite a few children scampering about on both sides of the river. The guards paid no attention to them at all.

A boy started crossing the river in front of me. The guards didn't do anything. I kept waiting for them to take action, but they didn't react at all. He was carrying an object above his head so it wouldn't get wet, but the water was only up to his waist. He got to the other bank after only a few moments and gave the object to a man who was waiting for him. The man took it and promptly disappeared, but the boy sat down on the riverbank and started smoking a cigarette, job done.

It seemed that crossing the river was a pretty easy affair.

I decided to move on. If I stood looking at the river much longer, the guards would surely get suspicious. Just as I started to walk away, one of the guards yelled, "Get back!" I was so jumpy, I thought he must be talking to me, so I stopped and turned around very slowly.

The woman who was washing some clothes was hurrying to step back. She was the one the guard had been yelling at. It seemed that the children had no problem crossing the river, but adults could only go out a yard or so.

I returned to the riverbank that night and hid under a bush to observe what happened after dark. The guards were patrolling with flashlights. Worse still, the moon was out. I could see its reflection in the river. It was far too bright to attempt a crossing, so I made my way back to the train station area.

There was a long bench at the station where people would sit to wait for their train. When I noticed people snacking, I stood or sat nearby and waited for them to throw the remnants of their food away. After grabbing whatever I could, I crawled under another bush and hid myself. I knew I'd never be able to get across the river in broad daylight without being seen. And after dark, it was just too bright because of the moonlight and the guards going round with their flashlights.

I didn't know what to do next. The only thing I could think of was to try to cross when one set of guards was handing over to the next. But how was I supposed to figure out the guards' routine without giving myself away? I mulled this question over endlessly in my mind as I lay awake on the cold ground.

It took me two more days of surveillance to figure out the best time to cross the river. By then, I was physically very weak. And of course my nerves were on edge. I kept checking my back whenever I walked anywhere. I got so paranoid, I thought everyone I passed was a policeman.

Eventually, I gave myself a stern talking-to. *Look! You don't have time for this. Your family's starving! You are getting weaker by the day. You have to get across that river! Otherwise, your whole family will die, and so will you.*

On the third night, I went back to the riverbank just after sunset and hid myself under the bushes, waiting for my chance. The guards were prowling around.

I can't be shot! I can't die here! I thought.

But I couldn't concentrate properly, so I lay down on the ground and closed my eyes. When I tried to stand up, I found I didn't have the energy to lift myself up. I thought this was it, that I was dying. I had made it so far; I was so close, but I had waited too long. And suddenly, the faces of my mother, my father, and all of my children came to my mind. My mother said, *You have to stand up and go! You must find the strength.* And then it started drizzling. I could feel the drops on my face. I opened my eyes, but I couldn't see properly through my tears. I turned my face to the sky. It was totally dark. Pitch-black. The rain grew heavier, and, strangely, my strength returned and my mind grew clear. *I must go,* I thought. *I must go now. Otherwise, I'm going to die here.* It was no longer just drizzling. It was a torrential downpour. Ten, twenty minutes later, I stood up and looked at the river. It was unrecognizable. Totally transformed. In that brief time, it had become a raging torrent.

I waded through the mud, toward the water.

What difference does it make? I get shot . . . I commit suicide . . . I stay here and starve . . . I die. So if you wanna shoot me, just do it, then! I thought as I tried to summon the courage to act.

I started walking along the riverbank. I didn't care anymore about the guards behind me. If anything, I actually *hoped* to die.

Something cracked under my foot. A twig? A root? Convinced I was about to be shot, I instinctively looked back. And to my astonishment, there wasn't a single guard in sight. Were they handing over to the next watch?

Yes! It was now or never. I threw myself into the river and started to swim. But then my head crashed into something. A rock? I have no idea. Water flooded into my mouth, and I was vaguely aware of being swept downstream. Then I lost consciousness.

I have no idea how much time passed. When I came to, I found myself lying on the riverbank.

Shit! I didn't make it across, I thought.

I was shivering uncontrollably, my strength completely gone. I managed to raise my head, and when I did, I saw a light in the distance. It seemed to be coming from a house.

How strange to turn on the light. Who would do such a thing? I wondered. Turning the light on at night in North Korea was tantamount to high treason. I couldn't stand up, but I found I could move enough to crawl. So I crawled toward the house with the light on.

Then I heard barking in the distance.

I must have drifted off, but when I woke up, a man I didn't know was carrying me on his back. I couldn't speak. I tried, but my lips refused to move. My vocal cords seemed to be paralyzed. I couldn't even grunt. I tried to move my fingers. Nothing. But wait. I *could* move my eyeballs. Where was I? I tried to look around.

Bushes. A dog. What was it doing, leaping about like that, racing around this strange guy's feet? Wagging its tail. Barking.

The man started talking to it. What was he saying? I couldn't make it out.

I tried once again to say something. But I still couldn't get a sound out. I tried again. Nothing.

The man kept on talking to his dog, in a kind voice.

And suddenly, it came to me. People didn't keep dogs in North Korea. They ate them. This dog was a *pet*. This wasn't North Korea. It was China. I'd made it. I couldn't believe it. It was nothing short of a miracle.

Despite my excitement, I was overcome by fatigue.

I fell asleep.

Born again.

When I woke up, the man was watching over me. I wanted to explain who I was, to thank him for his help, but I still couldn't speak. I tried to sit up, but he stopped me.

"It's okay. You need rest. Try to sleep," he said.

Later, he fed me rice gruel. He lifted the bowl and put the spoon to my lips.

If I'd had the strength, I'd have wept at his tenderness.

The gruel made me dizzy. I hadn't eaten for so long, my body couldn't take it. I felt as if I'd knocked back a bucket of alcohol.

I fainted.

I drifted in and out of consciousness for two days. I don't remember anything about it. But then, on the third day, I woke up feeling full of energy. It was strange. I mean, I didn't exactly leap out of bed, but I suddenly found I could stand up; I could walk. I looked around, gradually taking in my surroundings. I saw a TV, a fridge, a washing machine, a sofa bed, a motorbike, and a bicycle too. Unimaginable luxuries.

The man who'd rescued me came in. He was an elderly Korean named Kim, and he was the kindest person I've ever known.

I explained my situation in all its complexity.

"I'm not Korean. I'm Japanese. I'm trying to get back to Japan. I have to rescue my family. Can you help me?" I asked.

He took a puff on his cigarette. "You can't even get to South Korea nowadays. But *Japan*!" he said.

He told me about other people who'd escaped from North Korea. Not Japanese, of course. Native North Koreans. I was stunned when he told me what had happened to them. Even if they made it to the South Korean embassy in Beijing—no small feat, when you think of the distance and dangers involved—they were given the cold shoulder.

They were told, "We don't want to damage our relationship with China. I'm afraid we can't help you. You're on your own." In other words, do us a favor and get lost.

After the Korean War, China and North Korea had a "friendship signed in blood" in which they agreed to a "Border Security Cooperation Protocol." Fancy words for a simple process: if you escaped from North Korea but your luck ran out and you got caught, you were sent back.

Cue the firing squad.

As for South Korea, trade with China was all that mattered. That was evidently far more important than helping your own brother.

But Kim was all right. He was a good man, and I trusted him completely.

"Let me talk to my sons and some friends I can trust. I'll sort something out. Don't worry," he said.

I looked around and wanted to weep at what I saw. The telephone on the table. A radio. Some fruit in a bowl. The dog snoozing by the window. Compared with North Korea, this was Shangri-La.

After a while, Kim returned with two men in their forties who turned out to be his sons, Chorusu and Choro. To me, they looked incredibly wealthy in their smart, tailored clothes and their Japanese watches. Like their father, they traded flour, rice, and other staples with North Korea.

That was the legal side of their business. They also traded stuff that was under embargo—silver, antiques, and the like.

"I buy up old Japanese money that was used in the colonial era and sell it to a Japanese collector. He can't get enough of it. Suits me!" explained Chorusu.

They said they traded farther upstream, where the river was narrower. Luckily for them, the younger brother, Choro, used to work for the Security Service, and some of his friends were still members. So he knew how they operated, which was useful. He suggested I keep moving around. Which was exactly what I did. I stayed with him, his brother, his father, trusted friends.

Chorusu's house seemed like paradise, with all its electrical appliances, the mountains of white rice and pork, and fellow traders who were constantly stopping by to play cards. Everyone was smoking and gambling and having a good time. They all called one another "buddy" or "bud" or "pal." It took me back to my Korean junior high school days in Japan. It was clear to me that they respected Chorusu. And because I was his guest, they were always very polite and kind to me, which was quite a refreshing change. I felt guilty about enjoying these luxuries when I thought of my family back in North Korea, but I knew that if I was going to have any chance of helping them, I needed to get my own strength back first.

After a few days, I suddenly got the idea to call the Red Cross in Tokyo. Just like that, a memory came to me from way back in the eighties, of a man who had written to the Red Cross to help him get in touch with lost relatives in Japan. A little while later, he received a response, a "Tracing Request Form." The man was so happy to get a response that he showed the form to anyone who cared. I caught a glimpse of the address and phone number when he showed it to me, and I thought, *Wait a minute! This could be useful.* So I memorized the information on the spot. I can remember it to this day.

I asked Chorusu how to make an international phone call. Then I picked up the phone and dialed. I held my breath as I listened to endless clicks and buzzes.

But it worked. Someone answered. A female voice.

I couldn't understand a word. It was Japanese all right. But it had been so long. I was rusty.

"I'm Japanese. I'm in China. I go to North Korea with my family. Long time ago. 1960. I come back to Japan. I beg you." It was all I could say.

So I said it again and again.

She couldn't understand what I was saying. But she had the sense to put me through to another department.

"How can I help you?" a man asked.

Suddenly I could speak a little more clearly. My Japanese was coming back to me.

"My name is Ishikawa. I'm a Japanese citizen. My father was Korean. My mother Japanese. Way back in 1960, my father was conned into taking us to North Korea. We were promised a new life in a paradise on earth. The Japanese government was all for it. The United Nations knew all about it. Your charity was happy to supervise the greatest mass migration in the history of the world. Have you any idea what you did to us? You consigned us to a living hell. I've finally escaped. No one else has. I'm the first. The rest of us are dying or dead. It would be nice if you could help me get home." It all came pouring out of me.

Silence.

I've gone too far, I thought.

But then he spoke. And he sounded troubled.

"Okay. Please wait a moment. I'll call the Red Cross in China," he said.

A kind but ludicrous response.

"Are you out of your mind? If you do that, I'm a dead man."

I pointed out to him that the Chinese authorities wouldn't care what the Red Cross had to say. They'd just send me back, and I'd be shot.

He finally understood how difficult my situation was.

"Okay. I'll call the Ministry of Foreign Affairs right now," he said.

I gave him Chorusu's number, thanked him, and hung up.

To give the man his due, he moved very fast. About a quarter of an hour later, I got a call from someone in the Northeast Asia Division of the ministry's Asian Bureau, who told me to call the Japanese embassy in Beijing. They were expecting to hear from me.

I dialed the number he'd given me and told my story again.

"And you're definitely a Japanese national?"

I gave him my details. Date of birth. Place of birth. The precise date I'd been shipped off to North Korea. There had to be records.

Okay. He'd report to his boss and get back to me.

Everyone seemed to doubt that I was genuinely Japanese. Looking back on it, I can't really blame them. I could barely speak the language, after all. But I was scared to death of being arrested at any moment and felt like time must be running out for my family back in North Korea. I had no time for sympathy. I needed someone to help me get back to Japan, so that I could start working on helping my children.

According to Choro, phone tapping was par for the course near the border. It wasn't just a question of monitoring escapees. There were Russian and South Korean spies in the area too, looking for defectors or investigating suspicious activities. I decided it would be best to decamp again.

For the next few days, I moved from house to house. I kept calling the embassy, and they referred me to the Japanese consulate in Shenyang.

"Be patient," they said. "We're trying to get in touch with your relatives in Japan." But my patience was running low.

Finally, they succeeded.

"Congratulations. You're clear," they told me.

By this time, I'd been in China for a week, living in a state of terror that I'd be arrested at any moment. So I phoned the consulate in Shenyang and said I couldn't wait any longer.

"Okay, then. You need to come to Shenyang. Ask the people who've been sheltering you to bring you here. We'll pay them for their trouble. There's a huge TV transmission tower with a bridge right in front of it. Be there the day after tomorrow at five o'clock in the afternoon. Have you got that?"

I hung up and turned to the brothers.

"You've gone far beyond the call of duty, but I need to ask you one last favor. It's a big one. Can you get me to Shenyang? The consulate will cover your expenses," I said.

Choro didn't hesitate for a moment. "Sure. When do we leave?" he asked.

It was all I could do not to burst into tears.

"How about right now?" I asked.

We all laughed.

Chorusu got hold of a friend who had a car and asked if he could drive us.

He could.

The whole plan was in place before sunset.

Choro's wife was eager to come with us, so there were five of us in all.

I went to see Mr. Kim Senior before I left. I couldn't thank him enough for all he'd done for me. The tears streamed down my face as I tried to express my gratitude. I knew I would never see him again, and that I would never be able to repay his kindness for saving my life.

Then the five of us piled into the car and set off.

Shenyang was about two hundred fifty miles away as the crow flies. To get there by car, we had to cross over the Changbai Mountains. We could make it in two days if we drove nonstop. The mountain roads were narrow and winding and dotted with checkpoints.

When our driver spotted the first checkpoint up ahead, he called out a warning to me. I dove down in the backseat and covered myself with a futon, my heart thundering in my chest. The Kim brothers sat on top of me.

I heard a soldier's voice. It sounded young and friendly.

"Where are you folks off to?"

"Visiting some relatives in Shenyang."

And that was it. The soldier didn't even ask to see our travel permit. He just let us through.

"We're clear," Chorusu said, moving off the futon.

I emerged from beneath it and sat up.

I was amazed we'd got through the checkpoint so easily. I couldn't help asking about it.

"Well, these soldiers, you see . . . They're all alone in these isolated checkpoints in the middle of nowhere for hours on end. They like human interaction."

After thirty-six years of living in North Korea, I felt as if I were on another planet.

We drove for two days almost nonstop. The odd toilet break. The odd nap. Nothing more. We got to Shenyang around two o'clock in the afternoon on the day of the rendezvous.

I'd never seen so many cars. They were everywhere, a great milling mass of them. But I could barely take it in. I was breathless with excitement, but also extremely nervous. There was a North Korean consulate in the city, after all. There were secret police.

We found the enormous TV tower. The man on the phone had been right. You couldn't miss it.

We parked the car nearby, got out, and walked toward the bridge. The Kim brothers walked on either side of me.

When we got to the bridge, I called the consulate on a public telephone. My hand was shaking as I put the receiver to my ear.

"Hello? This is Ishikawa. I'm at the bridge. I don't think we can wait till the time we agreed. Too dangerous. Maybe this call is being tapped. I don't want to get picked up. Please come and get me now."

I put down the receiver without waiting for a reply.

Chorusu said to me—and I'll never forget it—"Don't worry! If something happens, I'll risk my life to protect you."

I nodded, but I couldn't really concentrate. I felt as if everyone around me was a threat. I was convinced I'd be caught any moment. My heart was hammering. My throat was dry, and my palms were clammy.

Suddenly, someone called my name from behind me.

"Are you Mr. Ishikawa?"

I turned around to find two men in expensive suits standing before me.

"My name's Kusakari," one said. "I'm from the consulate. You've been through a horrendous ordeal. I salute you. Let's go!"

He took my arm, and we started to walk away.

The second man thanked Choro and Chorusu and handed over some banknotes. A real wad, from what I could see. I was relieved they were being compensated for all they'd done for me.

The brothers looked amazed.

"I don't know what to say. I can never thank you enough. Look after yourselves!" I said.

"Take care! Go well!" they called out. Then they waved. And that was it. They were gone forever.

We walked to the consulate, which was only about five hundred yards away, surrounded by four high walls. Fine by me. There were Chinese policemen standing in front of the gate, fully armed. We walked into the consulate at two thirty in the afternoon. I can't tell you what it felt like to be in there. My emotions were potent and mixed. Even in my relief and my giddy disbelief, haunting images of my children flashed through my mind. A sharp pang of guilt reverberated through me. It's never ceased.

I kept waking up in the middle of the night. The rational part of me knew I was safe. But I still had nightmares of being caught and arrested, and often awoke in a cold sweat, heart pounding. I was startled by the slightest sound—even a creak from the floor or the rustling of the branches outside. I was convinced that the secret police would come and take me away.

The consul was at a loss for words the first time he set eyes on me.

"My God! How could they treat you like that? You look like a skeleton," he said. His wife burst into tears when I told her that people were really starving to death. She'd heard the rumors, but the reality was much worse than she'd thought.

I'd never experienced anything like the room where I was put up. It had two comfortable beds and an en suite bathroom. It was from a world I could never have dreamed of when I was struggling just to stay alive. As the days went by, my emotions were all over the place. I was still in a state of shock and disbelief that I'd made it, that this room I was in wasn't just an elaborate hoax. And while I felt overwhelmed with relief at having made it this far, I was tormented by the thought of my children. All I could hear in my mind was them calling out to me, *Dad! Dad!* It was hard to enjoy the food that was put in front of me when I thought of them starving back in North Korea. I thought of how I used to sing with my children before bed each night. All three of them were very good singers. They could express their feelings when they sang. When they were singing a sad song, they sang it with tears. I can't think of that even now without starting to weep myself.

Two weeks passed. I was shaving one morning and noticed that the color was returning to my face and my cheeks weren't as hollow as they had been. For safety's sake, I was confined to my room. The chefs and maids weren't informed of my presence, as some of them could well have been undercover agents. There was also the possibility that someone might report me to the authorities. Because of that, we adopted a precautionary code. Five knocks on the door and I would open it up. Otherwise, I kept it locked. Only the Japanese staff knew anything about me.

The meals that were prepared for me were supposedly for the consul's wife. She pretended to eat them but then secretly brought them to me. God knows what she ate herself. I still remember those meals—they were out of this world. Well, at least to me they were. They were full of vegetables and meat. If I'd been presented with such things in North Korea, I would have wolfed them down, but I was so worried all the time that my appetite was poor.

When I looked out the window during the day, I could see men across the street. I was convinced they were secret police watching my window. And then I heard footsteps on the roof. Or thought I did. I told Kusakari about it. After that, he boarded up some weak points he claimed to have identified. I imagine he did it just to calm me down.

The consul tried to settle my nerves. "Don't worry! We'll get you back to Japan," he said. He sometimes took me to the recreation room after nine o'clock in the evening after all the staff had departed. The room had a karaoke machine and TV. He got ahold of a shogi board and said cheerfully, "Come on! Let's have a game!"

I didn't know what the consul and his staff were doing during the day because I couldn't leave my room, but I was pretty sure they were negotiating with the Chinese government in some way. And then the First Secretary from the Japanese embassy in Beijing turned up, so I was fairly sure I was right.

The First Secretary was a scholarly type. I asked him a few questions in order to better understand my situation, but he just replied, "Don't worry. Be strong!" Nothing more.

A few days later, he came to my room and gave me a document. "Read this and then sign it, please," he said.

The document was a personal letter from the Ministry of Foreign Affairs. **Do not tell anyone for a while that the Japanese government helped rescue you**, it said. Of course, I signed the thing on the spot, and the First Secretary went back to Beijing.

About a week later, I was summoned by the consul, and a photo was taken of my face. I was told it was going to be used for a passport.

I was worried that something was going on behind my back. I mean, of course I was happy about the passport. It was a very promising development. But why were the negotiations taking so long? I was convinced that they had run into difficulties of some kind.

That night, when I was playing shogi with the consul, I asked him about it. He'd given me some expensive French cognac, so I may have been more direct with him than was appropriate. But I was worried about my family and getting increasingly anxious about the future.

"When can I go back to Japan? I think it's time you told me," I said.

He stopped his hand midmove and looked at me.

"The Chinese government hasn't granted you an exit visa yet. But it's just a formality. The First Secretary's been trying his best to get it all sorted out. I'm sure the tide will turn in our favor soon. So don't worry! Relax!"

According to the Japanese government, people like me who'd moved to North Korea but not changed their nationality were still Japanese citizens. But the North Korean government had other ideas. According to them, all Japanese people who'd immigrated to North Korea were now, ipso facto, North Korean. From their point of view, I'd effectively been kidnapped by the Japanese government.

The First Secretary and the Ministry of Foreign Affairs had been insisting that I, Masaji Ishikawa, was a Japanese citizen, so the Chinese government had no reason to deport me to North Korea. That was the crux of the negotiations. The key point was to ensure that the Chinese government could save face.

A few days later, I was talking to the consul when a call came in from the First Secretary in Beijing. As the consul picked up the phone, he turned the radio up and then explained to me, "If I do this, they won't be able to eavesdrop."

After the call, he summoned all the people involved with my case.

"The Chinese government will turn a blind eye to this case. To be precise, they've decided it doesn't matter if Mr. Ishikawa leaves China without their permission. That's the good news. The *bad* news is, if he gets caught by the secret police or a spy, the Chinese government can't help him at all."

The First Secretary estimated that it would take a few more days to arrange a plane and finalize the negotiations. He said he'd contact us again in four days, at which point we should move to Dalian City, from where I'd fly out.

I couldn't agree with that. "If we move to Dalian after he contacts us and I get caught, the whole thing will fail. I really think we should move to Dalian now and wait for him to contact us there," I said. I thought the Chinese government was tapping the telephone line in the consulate, so if we made a move, the police would be waiting for us at whatever time we had agreed upon on the phone.

The consul considered what I said, glanced at the clock, and said, "Okay. Let's do it. Let's leave right now!" It was already after midnight.

The staff got busy with preparations.

The consul's wife gave me one of the consul's suits to wear. It was a beautiful garment. I'd never worn anything like it. Honestly, I'd never even *seen* anything like it. Though I realized later that it was not particularly stylish or top-of-the-line, to me, it felt like putting on a prince's garb. After I got changed, she gave me a bag with some other clothes.

We went down the stairs arm in arm. Some policemen were guarding the building, so she acted as if I were her husband. We walked around the garden slowly, like a devoted couple enjoying the night air. She was humming a song I didn't know. At first I wondered why she was singing, but then I realized it was because I was being too silent.

There weren't any stars, and the night was very still. Consumed by the thought of what lay ahead, I couldn't enjoy the moment. But I could see what she was doing. And she was brilliant. I mean, not only was she fooling the policemen; she was also trying to make me relax.

I was moved to tears.

On our second turn around the garden, she suddenly said, "Mr. Ishikawa, please go through to the garage. Safe journey!"

And with that, she pushed me through a door.

I couldn't understand what she was talking about. But I could hear the sound of car engines. And then I noticed a corner of the floor had been dug up. I climbed down the hole and found a tunnel just big enough to crawl through. I didn't need a guidebook. I just dropped to my knees and crawled forward as quickly as I could.

There were three cars waiting when I emerged from the tunnel. I heard a muffled voice call out from one of them.

The consul's voice.

I ran over to the car and leaped in.

Someone shut the door, and all three cars sped off in a convoy.

There were several checkpoints on the way to Dalian. As we approached each one, I stretched out on the backseat, hidden under a blanket. We ate in the car and stopped only for bathroom breaks. Our destination was a kind of liaison center for Japanese companies doing business in Dalian. Run by the Japanese government, it would provide me with decent cover. We finally made it to the liaison office the following evening.

I can't tell you how relieved I was to have escaped from Shenyang without being caught.

If you look at a map, you'll see that Dalian is to the west of North Korea. Whereas Japan, of course, is to the east. So strictly speaking, the hellhole that had ruined my life was still sitting there defiantly between the place where I found myself and the place where I wanted to be.

Even so, Dalian is a port where you can at least look out to sea, where you can see the vast horizon and the ships sailing off to freedom. So never mind geography. Cooped up there in that liaison office, unsure whether the Chinese authorities would actually allow me to leave, I focused on the sea. The thought of it nearby gave me hope and made me smile. Japan was just over the horizon.

The building was cold, even with the heat on, so we all camped out together in one room. That suited me fine. I felt safe, and it was good to have company. I could talk about my dreams for the future and my plans for helping my family escape.

"I want to get a job right away. I don't even care what it is. I'll do anything, and I'll work hard—I always have. I just need to save some money to get my family to Japan. That's why I'm here. That's what I've been risking my life for."

Everyone nodded and murmured their support.

The First Secretary arrived the next day. He was very surprised that we were already in Dalian. He worked the case hard, calling the embassy in Beijing, double-checking this detail, and underlining that point. His planning was meticulous. I could tell that he was dedicated to the task, and I felt totally safe in his hands.

When he came to see me the following morning, he was ebullient. He said we should pose for a photograph.

"It's all sorted out at last. But I have to warn you. If anything goes wrong, we've never heard of you. I'm sorry that's the way it has to be.

But don't worry. Nothing *will* go wrong. I've made absolutely sure of that. Let's get you ready to get out of here. But first let's take a picture we can look back on for the rest of our lives," he said.

I have that picture to this day. I look very nervous, but my eyes are shining. Sparkling with my future dreams.

Just after lunch, the consul came up to me and shook my hand.

"Are you ready?" he asked. I nodded, trying not to show how anxious I was.

He handed me something.

"Use this when you get to Japan. You might need it," he said.

It was five hundred dollars.

I hadn't ever held such a sum in my hands. I was stunned at his generosity, but there wasn't time for long expressions of gratitude. I stuffed it into my jacket pocket and murmured a quick thank-you.

"Okay, everyone. It's time. Let's go!"

We piled into the waiting cars that whisked us off to the airport about fifteen minutes away.

I could see the terminal building up ahead. I couldn't see any planes, but I could hear one coming in to land.

When I was just about to open the car door, the First Secretary grabbed my hand.

"No talking from now on. Okay? Just follow me. Don't say a word!" he said.

As soon as I got out of the car, the consular staff surrounded me and swept me into the airport lobby. Everyone was moving very purposefully. Very fast. No looking around.

People heading in the opposite direction stopped to stare. I imagine we were a pretty strange-looking group.

Passport control? Forget about it. We went straight to the departure gate. I still have that passport I didn't have to show. It was stamped by the consul in Shenyang, to be used by November 11. Single use. It showed I had arrived in Narita. There was a stamp to prove it. But where was I traveling from? It was a mystery. A blank.

Once I reached the gate, a wave of relief swept over me. It was obvious the whole thing was being stage-managed. The Chinese government was in control. I would soon be on my way.

We walked out onto the runway. It was cloudy. Cold. I could see a big airplane in front of me with silver wings.

I climbed the steps with the First Secretary. When I reached the door, two women appeared in front of me. Flight attendants. All smiles.

"Welcome back!"

I peered into the plane. There was no one on board. It was a charter. Just for us.

I turned back to say goodbye, and the consul and his staff were all waving at me. I tried to say, "Thank you," but I couldn't get the words out because I was crying like a baby.

The flight attendants took me to my seat. I buckled my seat belt. The engines began roaring, and the plane started to move. Soon we were thundering down the runway. My stomach plummeted as the plane took off.

It was the evening of October 15, 1996. The plane touched down in Tokyo a short while later. I was back in Japan.

It took me thirty-six years to get home, but I finally did it.

EPILOGUE

So there I was. Born again. Again. But how did I feel? Overwhelmed by complex emotions. As I looked out the window as we came in to land, I could hardly believe the sight of my home country. All the lights glittering below looked like jewels. I was elated to be returning at last, to be putting the hell of North Korea behind me, to have a chance at creating a future of my own design. After so many years of helplessness and despair, I would finally be able to do something for my family. Those sparkling lights gave me a surge of hope. I would do whatever it took to get my family out of North Korea. It was difficult for me to think of what they must be enduring, but I let myself imagine the moment when we would all be together in Japan.

But my dreams were to be shattered once again. And now? Now I have just one thing left. My only true possession. I'm sorry to say that it's bitterness. Bitterness at the cruelty of life.

When I got back to Japan, the Ministry of Foreign Affairs arranged for me to be put up for the first few days in various hotels in Tokyo. The First Secretary stayed with me for a couple of days, but he soon had to get back to his job in Beijing. A man by the name of Matsui replaced him. Matsui, who served as the deputy director of the Asia and Oceanian Affairs Bureau, Northeast Asia Division, helped me move into a weekly apartment. Then he was gone, and I was alone, completely alone.

One day, Matsui came to see me. He asked me about the food situation in North Korea. But he didn't ask me anything about any of the other so-called returnees, and he didn't ask me anything about my family. Of course it was my family I wanted to talk about most. I hadn't escaped from North Korea just for myself. The whole point was to get my family out. To me, if they couldn't get out, my efforts had been a waste of time.

Matsui was then sent to Beijing to take over from the First Secretary. So then I had a new handler. He took me to my local ward office to help me get my residence card and so on. After that, he took me to an institution.

"This is where you'll be living from now on," he told me.

It was a rehabilitation center under the jurisdiction of the Ministry of Health, Labor, and Welfare, full of alcoholics and people too sick to make a living. It was called Hamakawa, located in the Shinagawa ward in Tokyo. What a place.

I was frustrated, to put it mildly. Why was I being treated like I was ill? We were wedged in, four people to a tiny room with only curtains as partitions. There were drug addicts shaking with full-body tremors as they went through withdrawal, tattoo-covered people muttering to themselves all day and all night. I would have felt sorry for them if I'd had the space in my mind and heart for such things. But I didn't. I was just desperate to find a job and earn a living, and angry about anything that stood in my way.

But then something incredible happened. After a few days, the media started contacting me—people from the newspapers, including the *Mainichi*, the *Yomiuri*, the *Japan Times* . . . I had no idea how they had heard about me. The only people who were supposed to know I'd come back to Japan were a few individuals in the Ministry of Foreign Affairs and a few others at the Immigration Bureau. I panicked and contacted the First Secretary, except he wasn't the First Secretary any-more. By this time, he was working at the Asia Pacific Bureau.

He was shocked when I told him what had happened.

"Christ! If it gets out that the Japanese government helped you, we'll all be fired. Please don't talk to anyone," he begged.

I appreciated everything that the ministry had done for me, so obviously I wasn't going to start talking to journalists. But then a member of parliament said he wanted to meet me. He was connected to a parliamentary committee that had worked on a North Korean abduc-tion scandal when a number of Japanese citizens had been kidnapped, drugged, and whisked off to North Korea.

I decided to go see him in the hope that maybe, somehow, he could pull some strings and help get my family out.

He was frank and friendly. "I just wanted to meet you. You've lived through quite an ordeal, haven't you?" he said.

I kept waiting for him to tell me what he wanted from me—or to give me a chance to talk about my family. But he had little to say except, "Good luck!"

After thirty minutes, I left.

Then I got the chance to meet another member of parliament, but he too ignored my pleas for help. Even worse, I could tell that he didn't want to get involved in any way.

They all seemed to be the same. I was shocked to realize that they just weren't interested in North Korea. I kept trying to make my case for my family, but it all fell on deaf ears.

After a year, I left Hamakawa. The truth is I never succeeded in finding a decent job. I tried everything, but it wasn't easy. I hated that I'd been reduced to living on welfare and that I couldn't send anything to my wife and children, but I wasn't exactly an ideal candidate. Just imagine what my résumé looked like. Educational background? Tricky one, that. Work experience? You really want to know?

I once got a job in a cleaning company. On my résumé, I claimed to have returned from South Korea, following the First Secretary's advice. Trouble was, people asked a lot of questions. What was South Korea like? What was this like, what was that like? Well, I'd never been there, so of course I couldn't answer. Gradually a rumor spread that I was a North Korean spy, so I eventually had to leave.

After that, I went to many job interviews, but I failed every one of them because of the bad economy, my age, my unclear background, and who knew what else.

In addition to my work status, I had to endure another source of grief, a much more personal one. The Ministry of Foreign Affairs tracked down my mother's relatives, but nobody wanted to see me. When I phoned one of my cousins, he suggested that we meet up. But the second time I called, he told me not to call him again and hung up on me. He probably thought I was going to ask him for money.

So no job. No family. No friends. Sure, I was glad to not be starving anymore. But it was hard being all alone. It was hard to feel so abandoned by a government that was well aware that we were practically browbeaten into emigrating. Still, they claimed that because we left of our own free will, we were not eligible for support or help.

One day, I was penniless and so desperate that I phoned the First Secretary.

"I need your help," I said.

"I can't meet you. I'm too busy. The Japanese government made sacrifices for you. You need to understand that. You need to find a way to live on your own and support yourself," he said.

I really wanted to say, "Have you ever built a shack with your bare hands? Have you hauled your mother's corpse up a mountainside? Have you struggled to survive on a diet of weeds?"

But it wasn't his fault. He was a good man at heart. He just didn't understand.

The first Inter-Korean Summit took place in Pyongyang in June 2000. The Japanese media said it marked "progress toward North-South reconciliation."

Forget about the missiles.

Forget about the violation of territorial waters.

Oh, and we got it wrong about Kim Jong-il. Maybe he isn't so bad after all. It was time for us to "modify our views."

I saw the pictures of Kim Jong-il talking to Kim Dae-jung, the president of South Korea. They were all over the television at the time. But I couldn't bear to watch.

Every day, I thought of my family still struggling to survive in North Korea. And countless others like them, slowly starving to death. I spent many nights lying awake, tormented by visions of them.

Kim Jong-il's hold on power was tenuous at best. After the death of Kim Il-sung, the leading members of the party changed allegiance and took off to South Korea. And then the leading members of the military who were close to Kim Il-sung disappeared too. Kim Jong-il knew all the talk of unification was just a farce. He cared only that he was on the world stage and that he was finally being taken seriously.

"A country may be destroyed, but its mountains and rivers will always remain." I'd always taken this expression to mean that, whatever happens, the scenery of your spiritual home will never change. But I was wrong. Or rather, the expression was wrong. After I returned to Japan,

I visited the town where I was born. I yearned to regain a sense of belonging, and I thought that the once-familiar scenery would bring back some sweet memories of my childhood and help heal my pain. But no. The town had become unrecognizable. And the scenery that I thought would comfort and console me had vanished. I'd lost not only my country, but also my birthplace. And so here I remain, in a place where I don't belong.

In a sense, I still don't even exist; I remain in limbo between two worlds. The Japanese government still hasn't officially admitted that I ever returned to Japan at all. So here I am, officially "not living" here. A life of "not living." That seems to be my curse.

Though my life is far easier in terms of survival, I remain haunted by very simple things. When I'm eating something considered a basic food in Japan—far simpler than anything most Japanese people eat, plain rice, let's say—I look at it and wonder how many meals it would provide in North Korea. And not just how many meals, but how many days of meals. The trouble is, such thoughts make it impossible for me to eat because my heart swells with grief. So when I feel that way, do you know what I do? I go to the ocean and toss the rest to the seagulls. I want to give this food to my family in North Korea. But I can't. So I entrust it to the seagulls. And in my heart, they carry it off to my family. And I weep.

I learned from a letter long ago that my wife had died. She was buried on a mountainside in Hamju. The last letter I received from Myong-hwa came in the autumn of 2005.

Help me! I want to live with you. I have absolutely nothing. I have two children. One son is two years old, and the other is five years old.

I was frantic; I didn't have enough money to send to her at the rate I was working, so I immediately looked for another job and found one as a cleaner in a place near Tokyo Tower. I worked there for one month, long days from five a.m. to one a.m., and as soon as I received my pay, I went to the Tokyo post office to send her one hundred thousand yen. Later, I received a letter from Ho-son. He informed me that she had died of starvation. She was in her late twenties. The money I sent was too late to help her. I last heard from Ho-son in 1998; the last news he sent was that Ho-chol was looking for work in a coal-mining area with his four children. Then the letters abruptly stopped. I haven't slept more than a few hours at a time since then. I still hope to rescue my remaining children. It is a terrible curse to not even know if they are still alive. But I believe they are. I have to believe so; otherwise, I couldn't go on.

I often think about what would have become of me if I'd stayed in North Korea. I would probably have starved too. But at least I'd have died in someone's arms with my family gathered around me. We'd have said our goodbyes. What chance of that now?

People talk about God. Although I can't see him myself, I still pray for a happy ending.

ABOUT THE AUTHOR

Photo © 2016 Hisanori Niizuma

Born in 1947 in Kawasaki, Japan, Masaji Ishikawa moved with his parents and three sisters to North Korea in 1960 at the age of thirteen, where he lived until his escape in 1996. He currently resides in Japan.